IT'S NEVER BEEN EASY

D0230974

IT'S NEVER BEEN EASY

Essays on Modern Labor

David Macaray

© Copyright 2009, David Macaray. All Rights Reserved

It's Never Been Easy
Copyright © 2009, David Macaray, All Rights Reserved.
Digitally authored and printed in the
United States of America. No part of this book may be used or reproduced in any
manner whatsoever without written permission except in compliance with
Fair Use provisions of U.S. copyright laws using brief quotations embodied
in critical articles, reviews and for journalistic purposes.

New World Digital Publishing
It's Never Been Easy

All rights reserved under United States and World copyright protection.
Published Worldwide by New World Digital Publishing
www.nwdigitalinc.com

Los Angeles, California, USA.

Copyright © 2009
ISBN 978-0-9825314-2-6

AUTHOR'S NOTE:

Most of the labor essays included here were written over the last seven years and appeared originally in various publications, including CounterPunch, The Exception Magazine, Liberalati, Los Angeles Times, Philadelphia Inquirer, State of Nature, and Synthesis/Regeneration.

This book is dedicated to working men and women everywhere, but particularly to the members of America's labor unions—those individuals who carry out the work, solve the problems, make it happen, but who, alas, rarely share in the treasure or glory. My thanks to Alex Cockburn, Jeff St. Clair, Marilyn and Valerie.

David Macaray
August, 2009

CLASS WARFARE IS ALIVE AND WELL

"Unlike the Europeans, Americans have
never hated the rich, only envied them."
—Gore Vidal

There was an experiment conducted by sociologists some years ago that endeavored to gauge people's sensitivity to "class." The experimenters set up two cars—a shiny new Cadillac, and a beat-up old Ford station wagon—at a traffic intersection. The drivers of both cars were instructed not to move when the light changed to green, but to wait for the car behind them to honk their horn.

They then timed how long it took for the motorist behind each vehicle to begin honking. The results were revealing. The experimenters found that the overwhelming majority of motorists began honking at the "poor" car almost immediately. By contrast, these same motorists waited, on average, *more than twice as long* before honking at the "rich" car.

So what did this prove? Well, because the experiment was done pseudo-scientifically, it didn't really *prove* anything. It was what it was. But if we want to extrapolate and go out on a limb, we could say that it exposed people's deep-seated contempt for those of lesser economic means and, by extension, those belonging to a "lower class."

After all, it can't be denied that instead of cutting the guy in the beat-up car a little slack, the drivers did the exact opposite. By honking their horns they engaged in the automotive equivalent of scolding, of chastising another driver, and, significantly, they did it far quicker to the "poor" person than to the "rich" one, thereby revealing a sense of class superiority.

Would it be wildly reckless to suggest that what was displayed in the traffic experiment is the same dynamic underlying the public's disdain for groups like janitors, nursing assistants and sanitation workers when they seek higher wages?

When people drive by and see striking janitors marching in front of an office building, carrying placards and demanding $14 dollars an hour, they don't automatically root for these workers. Rather, they tend to be annoyed or disgusted by the unseemliness of the public spectacle. Unskilled workers demanding $14 (which, by the way, if they work 40 hours a week, 52 weeks a year, computes to $29,120). How dare they?

Yet, when these same people read about hedge fund managers making, literally, hundreds of millions of dollars in a single year through the exotic and complicated manipulation of euros, dollars, yen and what have you, they don't so much as bat an eye.

We're willing to give the wealthy investment banker every consideration, but when it comes to people who work for a living—who do something we can actually *understand*, such as mop an office floor—we look down on them. And this is more than simply "rewarding" one for having put his college degree to work. It's a class judgement.

The extent to which people resist this notion, who adamantly deny that class distinctions exist in the United States, is as astonishing as it is disappointing. People bristle when you mention "class." To many, it smacks of an ideology vaguely Marxist in nature. It's as if admitting that class distinctions exist somehow detracts from our heroically egalitarian Land of Opportunity image.

But, in truth, we're as class-conscious in our own way as people were in Victorian England. Only we're less confident, less comfortable with it, more willing, in fact, to go to extraordinary lengths to convince ourselves that we're immune to such distinctions, because deep-down we think class divisions are somehow un-American. (Didn't Tocqueville make this same observation?)

In any event, this bias is something that labor unions such as AFSCME (American Federation of State, County and Municipal Employees) routinely encounter in their negotiations with management. The recent 5-day strike AFSCME called against the University of California (which occurred in late July) is a prime example.

The union had been working without a contract for almost a year before resorting to their symbolic strike. It should be mentioned that these AFSCME members aren't fiery-eyed radicals or militants; they're not the Longshoremen, for crying out loud. They didn't want to shut down. Indeed, the decision to stage their 5-day walk-out was made, more or less, reluctantly, out of desperation.

Incredibly, AFSCME wages are so low, that nearly *three-quarters* of the union membership qualify for food stamps or other government assistance. Moreover, the union is not seeking a gold-plated contract; it's merely seeking a decent one—one that will take full-time workers off the poverty rolls.

To no one's surprise, the UC regents don't see it that way. While college administrators have no problem justifying their $600,000 a year salaries, they can't bring themselves to pay their own employees a wage adequate to keeping them off welfare.

The reason they won't offer a higher wage isn't because the UC system can't afford it. Rather, the reason they won't offer it is because they don't believe these workers and their families *deserve* it. Let's put it another way: In the eyes of UC administrators, these workers deserve to remain poor. And if that ain't class warfare, what is it?

State of Nature
2008

SEVEN REASONS YOU SHOULD JOIN A LABOR UNION

One clue that this recession is going to be long and brutal is the fact that vocational guidance counselors are now suggesting to college graduates that they consider careers as open sea pirates. Okay, that's not true. But still, one can imagine how daunting and demoralizing things must be for college grads entering the job market at this precarious time—and not just for those who were hoping to break into investment banking, real estate or the stock market. Across the board, things are bleak.

And the situation is even worse for blue-collar workers, those entering the national job pool without benefit of a college degree. With most of the attractive manufacturing jobs having been dramatically downsized or exported, unless you can luck into a tech industry or land an apprenticeship in an established tradecraft, your choices are going to be fairly limited.

That's why, if you intend to be a blue-collar *worker* rather than a white-collar *careerist*, it's a smart move to consider becoming a union member. Here are seven practical reasons why.

1. Money. Let's deal with this one straightaway, and let's be sure to get it right. Generally speaking, union jobs pay significantly more than non-union jobs. From top to bottom, industry to industry, region to region, union wages are roughly 15% higher than non-union wages. It's as simple as that. If wages matter to you, then you'll want to join a union, because you'll make more as a union member. That's part of the reason companies resist having a union workforce. They don't want to part with that money.

Of course, you'll hear propaganda from anti-labor people about how that additional pay is going to be eaten up by monthly union dues, but that's a pathetic lie. Depending on the industry and geographical region, union dues run about $50-$60 a month, which is $600-$720 a year. And $720 isn't 15% of any union worker's income . . . unless he's earning $4,800 a year, which happens to be less than half the federal minimum wage, which means that whole "dues will neutralize any gains" argument is absurd.

2. Benefits. Pensions, medical insurance, paid vacation, holidays, personal holidays, sick pay, overtime premium pay, penalty pay and shift differential are generally not only better in a union shop, often the only way to obtain them is through a union contract. In truth, many of these benefits and perks don't exist without a union providing them. That's another reason why companies don't want to go union. Under a union contract they have to share those goodies.

3. Safety. This is a stark and sobering reality. The safety record of union facilities is demonstrably superior to that of non-union facilities. Anti-unionists can talk all they like about OSHA (Occupational Health and Safety Administration) being the "great equalizer," but it simply isn't true—no way, no how. Besides being understaffed and over-extended, OSHA has been effectively gelded by eight years of Bush administration anti-worker neglect and mockery.

A union contract gives employees the *immediate* right to insist on a safe work environment. Rather than having to petition a remote government agency in the hope that they come to your aid, as a union worker you can instantly *grieve* an unsafe condition. The safety provisions of a union contract guarantee immediate, hands-on control. It's no contest. Union facilities have an infinitely better safety record.

4. Dignity. As a union worker you don't have to put up with flaky bosses, arbitrary decisions, or co-worker harassment. You can still be fired for substandard work performance (as it should be), but you don't have to tip-toe around in fear or be at the mercy of weird or grossly incompetent managers. Because administering the provisions of a union contract requires a certain level of expertise, you tend to get better, more efficient bosses. Instead of flitting about making arbitrary, off-the-cuff decisions, they're forced to behave like "professionals."

5. Security. The boss can't walk up and fire you because he wants to give your job to his wife's nephew, who's looking for a summer job before returning to school. Management can't lay you off out of sequence. They can't demote you arbitrarily. Nor can they prevent you, without sufficient cause, from promoting to the next higher job when it's your turn. African Americans and women didn't get their fair shot at higher-rung manufacturing jobs until labor unions gave it to them, a fact that doesn't receive enough recognition.

6. Competence. Surprise! Union workers tend to be better workers than non-union workers. Just think about it: Which job in the community is going to attract a higher caliber performer—the one with the good wages, benefits and working conditions, or the crap job with low pay, lousy benefits and no air-conditioning? Not only will better workers apply to a union facility, but management will have a significantly greater number to choose from, allowing them to hire the very best.

7. Activism. You have the opportunity—the privilege—of one day becoming a shop steward, of representing your fellow workers, if they feel justified in giving you that responsibility. Shop steward is no glorified popularity contest, like being elected class president in high school. It's an important job. People on the floor are going to select the person they deem best qualified to represent their interests. As a union official, whose authority is recognized by federal labor law, you will forever be a footnote in the history of the American labor movement. Very cool.

CounterPunch
2008

UNION BUSTING IS ALIVE AND WELL

Established in 1982, with headquarters in tony Malibu, California, The Burke Group (after president and CEO David Burke) advertises itself as the world's largest management consulting firm specializing in "union avoidance and preventative industrial labor relations." Which is more or less a euphemism for "union busting."

The Burke Group (TBG, for short) earns its keep by defeating union organizing efforts. Torpedoing membership drives is their self-declared "specialty." When hired by a company to dissuade employees from joining a labor union, TBG representatives swing into action, utilizing every manner of high-powered, negative propaganda to make sure the referendum fails.

TBG's anti-union presentations (and, typically, there are several of them, spread over weeks) are conducted on company turf, where employee attendance is mandatory. Those who refuse to attend the presentations can be terminated.

Basically, what TBG does at these captive audience meetings is bombard the well-intentioned but impressionable employees with smears, innuendo, flattery, and scare tactics, using a standard, two-pronged assault: one-part economic and one-part psychological.

The economic part consists of pretending that, contrary to what they've heard, workers don't actually "gain" materially by joining a union. Any wage or benefit increase will, in fact, be eaten up by ever-increasing monthly dues that are used to pay the inflated salaries of greedy union bosses, and by debilitating strikes, where employees are thrown out of work for months at a time, with no say in the matter. That's their pitch.

Of course, these assertions are not only counter-factual and purposely misleading, they're downright insulting to anyone who's been paying attention. Union wages alone (not even counting benefits) are, on average, 15% higher than non-union wages. And, because dues run about $50-$60 per month, and amount to but a tiny fraction of that differential, the suggestion that higher wages will be off-set by monthly dues is absurd.

As for strikes, their impact is also wildly exaggerated. In truth, given the economic climate and status of organized labor, how many actual strikes are there anymore? The reason strikes make the evening news and front page of the newspaper is because they occur so infrequently; and the ones that last for "months" are rarer still.

Moreover, a union *cannot* raise the monthly dues without a majority of the membership voting to raise them. And federal labor law stipulates that voting on dues increases (as well as officers salaries) must be conducted by secret ballot. It couldn't be any clearer. Yet, these professional union-busters try to make it sound like joining a union means abandoning democracy and common sense, and placing oneself at the mercy of money-hungry despots.

The same goes for strikes. Because a strike is such a momentous undertaking, a union negotiating team cannot call one unless the membership has already given them authorization to do so. That stipulation is spelled out in the by-laws. Again, it couldn't be any clearer.

In fact, some unions, such as the Screen Actors Guild (SAG), require even more than a simple majority; they require a 75% mandate for strike authorization. In short, no matter what these union-busters claim, a union doesn't hit the bricks unless the members themselves choose to do so. Yet, companies like TBG continue to sell the idea that union members have no say in what happens to them.

The psychological part of the presentation is equally misleading. TBG reps try to convince employees that once they join a union they no longer have unrestricted or unimpeded access to management. They are told that, by virtue of signing up, they automatically define themselves as management's "enemy," and, accordingly, can expect the company to treat them with hostility and contempt.

The propaganda is unremitting. Workers are warned that, if they ignore the sound advice being offered them and choose, instead, to join a union, they will go from being free, self-sufficient and valued employees to mere foot soldiers in organized labor's vast army of minions. They paint an unbelievably demoralizing picture.

It's also not uncommon for professional union-busters to use visual aids. Typically, they'll show footage of downtrodden workers manning picket lines, union goons battling the police, and scowling, overweight union bosses doing the perp walk as they're led away by federal agents for violating racketeering statutes or stealing money from the union's treasury. Anything to make organized labor look bad.

As heavy-handed and coarse as these methods are, TBG has been surprisingly successful using them. Among its "victorious" customers are General Electric, Honeywell, Coca-Cola, the Eaton Corporation, Virgin Air, T-Mobile, K-Mart, and the Chinese Daily News. With TBG's help, all of these businesses were successful in keeping their employees from joining unions.

Because so many of the workers being targeted by organized labor these days are Latinos, many of whom are recent immigrants working at jobs at the bottom of the economic ladder, TBG has convinced employers that they need qualified Spanish-speakers to do their dirty work.. And TBG speaks fluent Spanish. (Their consultants also speak Tagalog, French, Portuguese, Vietnamese, and several dialects of Chinese.)

Indeed, TBG takes great pride in customizing its service. When the Chinese Daily News (CDN) came to TBG for assistance in crushing its employees' organizing drive, the firm chose as its representative one Larry Wong, an ethnic Chinese. They rarely miss a trick. Predictably, TBG's services don't come cheaply. According to reports, CDN alone has paid TBG more than $800,000 in consulting fees.

So next time people are tempted to criticize organized labor for not recruiting more new members, they should take a moment to consider the opposition. When it comes to keeping the unions out, American businesses are willing to pay cash. TBG is just one of many companies willing to accept it.

CounterPunch
2009

KEEPING UNIONS OUT: FEAR IS A WEAPON

As the late Senator Paul Wellstone liked to say, "We may be entitled to our own opinions, but we're not entitled to our own facts." Even with organized labor's many problems (shrinking membership, internal dissension, gutless Democrats, growing irrelevancy, etc.), there's no disputing the facts.

Fact: Across the board, union jobs pay more (10-15% more), offer better health and medical benefits, and provide workers greater on-the-job security and influence than non-union jobs. Fact: Union facilities are demonstrably safer than non-union facilities; statistically, the numbers aren't even close. Fact: If unions didn't represent a threat to management's greed and unchecked authority, they wouldn't be so vehemently opposed by businesses and business lobbies.

All of which raises the question: Given the post-Reagan assault on the earning power and dignity of blue-collar jobs, why aren't more people signing union cards? Why haven't the marginal and disenfranchised in the workforce wised up? Union membership used to hover at close to 35%; today it's barely 12%. Worse, if only private industry were counted, it's less than 7%. Better money, richer benefits, safer environment, more control . . . what's not to like?

The short answer is that forming a union shop can be a complicated, even dangerous undertaking. The site's employees not only require capable leadership, they need a plan of action and a cadre of dedicated "insiders" willing to sneak around and get 30% of the people to sign union cards (the minimum required by the National Labor Relations Board to sanction an election). And even after getting those signatures and filing that petition, there's a daunting up-hill struggle awaiting.

As for the "sneaking" part, while it's not required, it's strongly recommended. Ask anyone who's done it. When management gets a whiff of union cards being passed around, hackles go up, and they tend to punish the ringleaders, both as a practical matter and as a warning to future activists. They fire people.

The standard charge is "unsatisfactory work performance." When employees who are paid by the hour are caught passing out union literature (even on their coffee breaks), they're charged with "stealing" company time, and are terminated.

Because it's perfectly legal to circulate union literature on the job (so long as it doesn't "interrupt, restrain or restrict" the operation), punishing an employee for doing so is a violation of federal labor law. Companies realize this; they know it's a violation. It's just that successfully keeping out the union by any means possible falls into that category of the ends justifying the means.

Of course, the fired "instigators" are more or less dead in the water. Not yet being union members and, therefore, not having access to free legal counsel, they have little recourse but to fight for reinstatement on their own. Even if they do manage to get their jobs back, months or *years* later, the union organizing drive is likely to be ancient history.

In truth, intimidation and outright threats are common practices. The United Mine Workers is a prime example. Although the UMW has filed numerous ULPs (unfair labor practice charges) against coal companies, accusing them of coercing prospective members, the NLRB has seldom moved beyond a preliminary investigation. Even though, in fairness to the NLRB, charges of coercion are difficult to prove, the Board simply has shown little interest in taking on the big boys. This has been particularly true during the Bush administration.

According to Phil Smith, Communications Director of the UMW, coercion and intimidation are the main reasons why, even with the alarming safety record of non-union mines (92% of all coal mining fatalities since Jan. 1, 2006, have occurred at non-union sites), less than 30% of America's coal miners are unionized.

Coal miners are tough sons of bitches. Anyone who drills their way two miles into a mountain, and then sets up shop there, eight hours a day, has to be tough. But the threat of being black-balled by the industry or having the mine sub-contracted to an outfit that refuses to recognize the UMW (a common ploy, according to Smith) outweighs taking the chance of trying to join the union. Even tough guys fear losing their jobs.

When a company—any company—can't dissuade its employees from signing union cards, and a petition manages to get filed with the NLRB, the management team shifts into its Def-Con 4 mode. Human Resources team goes on full-alert. It's been said that companies react to a union membership drive the same way a Swiss housekeeper reacts to finding a rat in the pantry.

Let's be clear: If management didn't object to employees forming a union, they wouldn't force them to go the NLRB route in the first place. Instead, they'd agree to recognize them as soon as a majority of the employees (50% +1) signed cards. This method is known as the "card check" system. Once fairly rare, it's become increasingly common as union and community pressure has forced businesses to submit to democracy. But even with the card-check method, intimidation and disinformation still occur. Meanwhile, the old guard remains unmoved. Their view: If you want a union shop, you're going to have to do it the hard way.

It's after the cards are in, and the Board is notified, that the real fight begins. During the run-up to an election (which can take months to schedule if company lawyers use creative stalling tactics), management launches a zealous, anti-union campaign whose aim is to inundate the employees, break down their initiative, through terror, intimidation, flattery and bribery.

Wal-Mart comes to mind. They have surveillance cameras in their parking lots to protect employees from being intercepted by union organizers as they make their way to and from their cars. Wal-Mart employees are required to report any person they meet who tries to engage them in a discussion of labor unions, and are warned not to accept anything these people may try to give them. (Isn't this what we tell our kids about child molesters?!)

Typically, Wal-Mart's anti-union campaign will include everything from mandatory come-to-Jesus meetings where employees are "educated" about the evils of union membership (via movies, slide-shows and first-person horror stories) to the awarding of previously unannounced (surprise!) cash bonuses, as a token of management's appreciation of their work. That these cash gifts occur on the eve of a union certification vote is dismissed as coincidence.

Organizers in the field report the following (in no particular order) as the five most frequently used propaganda weapons used by management:

- Employees are told that any monetary gains will be wiped out by union dues, which run as high as $300-$400 per month, and can be raised at any time. Fact: While monthly dues vary from union to union, $50 is about average. And dues, initiation fees and officers' salaries can't be raised without the membership's secret-ballot approval. It's the law.

- Employees are warned that strikes will keep them out of work for months at a time, ruining them financially. Fact: While strikes used to be fairly common, they are now rare, especially the long ones. The recent strikes called by the UAW—against GM and Chrysler—lasted two days, and six hours, respectively. The WGA, which has been out for barely over two weeks, will be re-meeting with the AMPTP on November 26, with a chance of settling.

- Playing Mr. Nice Guy, management assures the workers that "carpetbaggers and opportunists" aren't necessary, that any safety or labor problems can be handled in-house. Fact: If that were truly the perception on the floor, the employees wouldn't be seeking union assistance.

- Employees are reminded that union bosses are corrupt, and that members aren't allowed a say in who gets elected. Fact: The Landrum-Griffin Act guarantees every member the right to vote. Even the Teamsters get to pick their leaders. Indeed, if American presidential elections were as openly democratic as union elections, we wouldn't still be flogging something called the Electoral College.

- Management threatens to shut down the operation and move away. It's an illegal tactic, but it's used nonetheless. Fact: Companies pull up stakes for lots of reasons, but having a union shop is rarely the determining factor. In today's climate, if a business can make more money by moving to Mississippi, India or Timbuktu, they'll do it . . . union or no union.

After considering the many obstacles placed in the way of joining a union, perhaps the question should be restated. Instead of asking why there aren't more people joining unions, the proper question should be: Given the hassles, threats and pitfalls awaiting them, how is any organizing drive *ever* successful?

CounterPunch
2007

15

ELEGY FOR LABOR DAY

Established as a national holiday in 1894, during Grover Cleveland's second administration, Labor Day was originally intended not only to honor American working men and women but to formally acknowledge the growing stature of the burgeoning U.S. labor movement.

Considering what's happened during the ensuing 114 years—the public's subsequent disillusionment with labor unions, coupled with the ability of special-interest groups to mobilize opposition, and the Democratic party's unreliability and gutlessness—it's highly unlikely that Congress could get the same holiday passed today. More to the point, it's doubtful its members would even bother to try.

How far to the right has the country tilted in just 40 years? Under the *Republican* administration of Richard Nixon, OSHA (Occupational Safety and Health Administration) became law, food stamps were expanded, federal wage-price controls were initiated, and the Clean Water Act was passed. Under the *Democratic* administration of Bill Clinton, NAFTA became law, the banking industry was deregulated, and social welfare was all but dismantled.

Not surprisingly, labor has been waylaid by the fallout. Unions have not only lost what remained of the charm and political utility that once sustained them, they've seen the one ideological bond that seemed indestructible—the support of the academic left—fray to the point of severing. While labor's relationship with the soft center of the Democratic party had always been tenuous and prickly, union dialecticians rejoiced in knowing they had academe solidly on their side.

That's all changed. Today, arguably, American academics have more sympathy for Palestinian suicide bombers and Acapulco cliff divers than for striking auto workers. Despite the occasional rhetorical flourish (usually heard around election time), America's politicians, mainstream media, general public and lefty academics now treat organized labor the way they

16

treat landfills, criminal recidivism, and radioactive waste—something they're forced to acknowledge but would rather not discuss.

According to myth, unions were, once upon a time, "legislated into existence" by a benevolent federal government. As the story goes (despite Labor Day's date of inception), organized labor didn't really arrive on the scene until after a New Deal Congress passed a series of federal laws to pave the way, the first of which came in 1935 in the form of the National Labor Relations Act, popularly known as the Wagner Act.

The Wagner Act established the NLRB (National Labor Relations Board) and guaranteed unions the legal right to organize, strike and collectively bargain. Wagner was followed by other landmark labor legislation, including the Fair Labor Standards Act (1938), Taft-Hartley Act (1947) and Landrum-Griffin Act (1959).

In truth, however, unions had been taking their cow to market—actively organizing and bargaining—for almost 150 years before any major legislation. Remarkably, by the early 1790s union "guilds" had already been well established in this country. There were bootmaker collectives in Philadelphia, tailors in Baltimore, and newspaper print-setters in New York City. As far back as 1825, hundreds of Boston carpenters went on strike for a 10-hour day, and in 1835, mill workers in Paterson, N.J., successfully struck for the 11-hour-day/six-day week.

In fact, the decades from the 1880s to the 1900s witnessed a tremendous surge in union membership (particularly in mining, textiles and trade crafts), including, interestingly, the establishment in 1885 of the Brotherhood of Professional Baseball Players, the first pro sports union in history.

But the government's "protective" New Deal legislation did leave its indelible mark. In one swift stroke, the Wagner Act co-opted the American labor movement, placing its holy trinity (organizing, bargaining, striking) under federal statutory control for the first time.

One doesn't need an AFL-CIO decoder ring to recognize that by removing labor disputes from the factory floor and the street, and placing them in the venue of the courts, the NLRB shifted the advantage to the party with not only the most money and prestige, but with the most to be gained by stalling tactics. Nothing has been the same since.

Today, while Canadian and European workers are free to join unions simply by signing membership cards, American workers, astonishingly, must petition their government for permission. The bureaucratic thicket created by the Taft-Hartley Act, passed by a Republican Congress over President Truman's veto(with help from the Democrats), has made becoming a union member more difficult than becoming a U.S. citizen.

In 1913, Supreme Court Justice Louis Brandeis said, "Labor cannot on any terms surrender its right to strike," and he was right. If Congress had been committed to leveling the playing field we would already have laws on the books, like those in Canada and Europe, making it illegal for striking workers to be permanently replaced by scabs. Realistically, what economic leverage do workers have when voting to go on strike is tantamount to giving up their jobs?

A bold proposal: Let us repeal Taft-Hartley, along with the minimum wage, and allow labor to compete in a "free market." If those free market worshippers mean what they've been preaching all these years about the infallibility of the free market, then let the American worker participate "freely" in that market. If joining (or withdrawing from) a union makes sense, then workers should be permitted to make that decision without government interference.

Conversely, if unions are exposed as the obsolete, parasitic institutions they're portrayed to be, then so be it; allow them to follow the dinosaur and Model T into extinction. But it should be the American worker—not Big Brother—who decides.

Los Angeles Times
2003

WHY WE SHOULD BAIL OUT THE AUTO COMPANIES

Let's put two things on the table immediately, two things which, while not exactly *logical*, are nonetheless *meaningful*. So, if you're looking for steel-trap logic or cold, bottom-line infallibility, you won't find them here. But if you're willing to consider a few realistic, peripheral considerations, some of this should make sense.

First, even though we're being bombarded on all sides with news of economic doom, let's not delude ourselves. The Big Three automakers aren't just another industry, so let's not pretend they are. Let's not pretend they're a chain of coffee joints or convenience stores, or even a big-time outfit like American Express, who, reportedly, is already sniffing around for some of that government money.

Detroit is different. Automakers are not only the largest manufacturing industry in the United States, they are, undeniably, the most glamorous, prestigious, loyal and uniquely *American* corporate enterprise in our history. They're Industrial America's version of the Liberty Bell, the Alamo and the Lincoln Memorial, all rolled into one. Smirk if you like, but it's true.

Americans shouldn't have to be reminded of our 100-year romance with cars, or the fact that it was we, the United States, who first mass-produced automobiles and introduced them to the rest of the world. And the world fell in love with American cars as a consequence. Pancho Villa drove a Ford Model-T. The Maharaja of Kapurtala (Punjab, India) drove a '59 Chevy Impala.

I bring this up only to establish the fact that when we talk about the auto industry, we're talking about a legacy enterprise, a cultural icon. And I'm saying that people who cavalierly assert that allowing one or more of the Big Three to go bankrupt don't have the first clue as to the enormity of what they're suggesting.

19

Besides the 240,000 people who work directly for Chrysler, General Motors and Ford, there are an estimated 2.7 million more who work in related industries, who supply parts, raw materials, sales and technical services. It's been predicted that a collapse of the auto industry could affect as many as 3 million people, a full 5% of manufacturing jobs in the U.S.

Second, if history doesn't matter, if this conversation isn't about what *was*, but about was *is*—if it's about money, and not cultural icons and such—then let's talk money. Indeed, if it's their hard-earned money that American taxpayers are concerned about, then fine, let's talk about that. Let's talk about how we spend it.

We've already blown close to a *trillion dollars* on an unwinnable war (not to mention the loss of life and destruction of a country), and continue to pour an additional *$14 billion a month* down that same bottomless rathole. On a dollar for dollar basis, this has been a monumental debacle, arguably, the greatest foreign policy blunder in our history.

Still, from what we're hearing, American taxpayers and their representatives are having a problem with giving $25 billion worth of economic relief to the struggling Big Three. They are objecting to this relief on the grounds that [drum roll] "it doesn't make good business sense." Please.

Not only have we had, literally, *billions of dollars* stolen from us by corrupt Iraqi officials and their political stooges, we've paid billions of dollars to Halliburton, Blackwater and scores of lesser known but equally greedy private contractors, all in the name of "patriotism."

Yet, given this record of pissing away money like drunken sailors, American taxpayers are now suggesting that it's time to get all stingy and wise and fiscally conservative, drawing the line at bailing out America's most hallowed industry—all in the name of "tightening their belt." If that's what's happening here, give me a goddamn break, people.

20

On the other hand, if this is about assurances or guarantees, that's a whole other deal. That's an eminently reasonable request, one we should pursue. Instead of giving away billions of dollars with no strings attached (as we're doing in Iraq), let's attach some economic and environmental requirements. Insisting that Detroit develop a car that gets 85 mph, with drastically reduced carbon emissions, would be a good start.

Let take this opportunity to reinvent the car business, but this time in the image we want. For crying out loud, we're the country that put a man on the moon and invented the reusable condom. Surely, we have the technical expertise and creativity to make a radically fuel-efficient automobile.

But it's also time we finally acknowledged the elephant in the room. That elephant is health care. The U.S. auto industry, which spends upwards of 30% of its payroll on employee health insurance (including premiums and administrative costs), competes with companies whose governments underwrite employee health care.

Even though labor costs account for, roughly, 8%-10% of the price of a new car, health insurance is killing the industry. Right out of the chute, before anything's been bought or sold, the Big Three is already thirty cents on the dollar in the hole. Given that crippling discrepancy, it's fairly amazing that Detroit has managed as well as it has.

Of course, the Republicans in congress—the same faux-patriots who prevented us from joining the rest of the industrialized world in obtaining national health care by waving the hysterical banner of "socialized medicine"—don't want to blame health insurance for contributing to the problem. Instead, they want to blame labor unions.

Instead of blaming Big Pharma and Big Insurance, they're blaming the UAW; they're blaming working people—people who are making $48,000 a year, hanging on to their middle-class identity by their fingernails, trying to make a living.

By bailing out the automakers (albeit with stringent conditions) we'll be saving one of America's truly valuable institutions. We'll be giving it a second chance. Twenty-five billion dollars is less than we spend in two months on this war. Doesn't Detroit deserve a small fraction of the "generosity" we're showing the Iraqis?

CounterPunch
2009

ORGANIZED LABOR ON THE ROPES

When an interviewer asked novelist Jane Bowles to sum up her philosophy of life, she replied: "Everything gets worse." With the Labor Day holiday focusing our attention on the historic achievements and sacrifices of working men and women, we are once again reminded of just how low the American labor movement has sunk, and may wonder if Bowles was right.

And nothing—no one single event—is more emblematic of labor's sorry state than its failure to organize Wal-Mart Stores, Inc. Not even the AFL-CIO's messy, on-going internecine dispute, embarrassing and potentially damaging as it is, can match it.

After years of intense, high-profile courtship and the expenditure of millions of dollars, the AFL-CIO—labor's version of the Pentagon—couldn't organize a single one of Wal-Mart's 3,600 stores in the United States. Not one. That's not just discouraging; that's scary.

Somehow, the giant retailer was able to convince its 1.2 million employees, the majority of whom are relatively underpaid and under-insured, that union representation would hurt more than help them. Granted, Wal-Mart used a potent combination of intimidation, disinformation and flattery to kill the membership drive; but in the end, it was the employees themselves who voted to keep the union out.

National politics is another disappointment. The Democratic Party, labor's natural ally and long-time benefactor, has all but run for cover. Apparently, being regarded as "pro-labor" is now a political liability.

Compare FDR's exuberant 1935 quote ("If I worked in a factory, the first thing I'd do is join a union") with John Kerry's sheepish performance in the 2004 presidential debates. For those keeping score, Kerry mentioned labor unions a grand total of one time—an off-handed reference to (of all things) the inevitability of U.S. jobs being lost to globalization.

So how, over the course of just a few decades, have unions gone from being respected and admired to being more or less reviled? After all, it was unions—not Congress, the church or philanthropic foundations---that mandated equal pay for women, maternity leaves, and the abolition of child labor, not to mention health care, pensions and paid vacations. What's not to like?

No one is naïve enough to expect a return to a 1930s mind-set. LIke Greece, labor had its brief, incandescent moment of glory, and, like Greece, it will have the rest of its history to mourn the loss. But labor's decline has left in its wake a negative perception that goes beyond America's reverence for individuality and mistrust of collectivism. Some disturbing myths have entered the national bloodstream.

Chief among them: (1) unions are undemocratic; (2) union workers are slackers; and (3) unions, while once useful, are no longer necessary. Let's take a closer look.

First, for the record, if presidential elections were as conspicuously democratic as union elections, we wouldn't still be flogging something called the Electoral College. Indeed, not only are most unions stubbornly democratic, the majority are virtual hothouses of grassroots participation. As mandated by the Landrum-Griffin Act (1959), elections are wide-open affairs, strictly governed by local bylaws.

Second, jobs that pay well, offer good benefits and provide decent working conditions (i.e., union jobs) typically attract higher caliber workers. The notion that the most desirable jobs in a community would be filled by deadbeats is ludicrous. In any case, no union contract has ever contained language prohibiting management from disciplining or demoting unqualified workers. Why? Because no union negotiator would dare suggest such a provision, and no manager would ever sign a contract that included one.

Third, with an estimated 30 million "working poor" in the country—employees who can barely afford rent, have no health insurance and, in many cases, qualify for food stamps and other poverty programs—how can anyone realistically suggest that labor unions are no longer necessary?

With the post-industrial landscape and global fallout so favorable to corporate interests, it's not surprising that management expects to run the table every time it picks up a cue stick. But isn't that all the more reason to embrace a defiant "loyal opposition"? Rather than asking if unions have outlived their usefulness, the more appropriate question is: Why aren't those marginalized Wal-Mart workers demanding to sign union cards?

Philadelphia Inquirer
2005

A BRIEF HISTORY OF UNION NEGOTIATIONS

To anyone curious about how labor and management actually conduct contract negotiations, they should know that, even though these things are wildly unpredictable and can change from courteous and productive to acrimonious and destructive in a heartbeat, the negotiating process itself adheres to a surprisingly conservative, rigid and time-honored format. I've been Involved in half a dozen of them. They've all been different and they've all been the same . . . even the ones that resulted in a strike.

The parties begin by setting a starting date, usually one well in advance of the contract's expiration; next, they have a preliminary meeting to lay out the ground rules and logistics (where they'll meet, what side of the table people will sit on, what time in the morning to begin, who pays for the coffee, etc.); next, they notify the FMCS (Federal Mediation and Conciliation Service), in Washington D.C, of their intention to bargain; and then, on the first day of official business, they formally exchange agendas, each of which has a Language and Economics section.

After that, the parties spend 99% of their time doing three things: meeting privately with their own committee members, discussing agenda items across the table, and exchanging written, initialed proposals and counter-proposals.

These three things can require as a little as a week or two, or as long, literally, as several months. Boiled down to its basics, a labor-management negotiation is a protracted argument over money. It's all about economics. Nothing more. Even the "language" items on the agendas have a cost attached to them.

Given the current predicament of organized labor, it's hard to believe that there was a time, not very long ago, when companies didn't even bother bringing an agenda to the table. They showed up naked. Unlike the union, which always (always!) brought along, an ambitious, detailed list of things it wanted to obtain, improve, overhaul, tweak or eliminate, it was not uncommon for companies to acknowledge that they were more or less satisfied with the way things were.

Until fairly recently, it was the union who was recognized as the "moving party," and the company who "fielded" the union's agenda. Indeed, if the union hadn't insisted on sitting down every couple of years and hammering out a new contract, most companies would've happily extended the existing agreement, with no questions asked.

Management was obliged to consider the union's list of requests for improvements in wages, benefits and working conditions—to consider them, discuss them, challenge them, deny most of them, and, ultimately, agree to accept just enough of them to avoid a strike. Traditionally, that's how bargaining was done.

By the late seventies and early eighties, this had all changed dramatically. And it was the Big Three automakers, more than any other industry, who led the charge.

America's on-going love affair with cars had not only made Detroit wealthier than it ever dreamed, it laid the groundwork for the UAW (United Auto Workers) emerging as the nation's most prestigious and influential labor union. When the economy was chugging along on all eight cylinders, it was the UAW, more than any union in America (including Hoffa's Teamsters), that represented the gold standard, and everybody tried to copy them.

Every union in America maneuvered to get a contract as sweet as the UAW's. The Auto Workers were the first big-time union to negotiate personal holidays and paid sick leave, the first to get shift differential and exotic overtime pay, the first to get cost of living allowances, medical insurance, company pensions, iron-clad seniority, and union-autonomous shop safety programs. The rest of organized labor followed their lead. It's been said that the UAW launched America's middle-class.

Of course, when the bubble burst, and the auto companies hit hard times, it was the UAW who paid the dearest price. Besides losing, literally, hundreds of thousands of members due to layoffs and plant closures, the UAW was attacked; the auto companies came at them with a vengeance. They renegotiated existing contracts, slashed wages and benefits, demanded exorbitant give-backs and concessions, and made sweeping, across-the-board changes in administrative rules and policies.

Worse, even after the auto companies had clawed their way out of the ditch and were once again making big profits, they continued their offensive. While part of their assault was old-fashioned payback, plain and simple, another part was the recognition that the labor climate in the country had drastically changed. Corporations now had the upper hand. They had unions on the run; not just the UAW, but virtually every union in America.

Companies that traditionally had signed two or three year contracts were now demanding four, five and six year deals, locking unions into punishing agreements that couldn't be changed for half a decade, and wage scales with no mechanism for keeping up with inflation. It wasn't simply the frills that were being removed from these contracts, it was their heart and soul and guts.

In other words, the roles had been completely reversed. Companies were now bringing their own ambitious agendas to the bargaining table, and daring the union to strike. These agendas were more extensive, more aggressive and predatory, than anything the unions had ever introduced. In a word, labor relations had been "reinvented."

Initially, organized labor was amenable. When the economy took a downward turn, the unions were smart enough to realize they had to open the door a crack and allow management to make the necessary adjustments. It would have been irresponsible and unrealistic to think otherwise. Still, given what they'd learned from a century of collective bargaining, unions remained wary and cautious, aware that the companies might use the extraordinary circumstances to do mischief.

But even with labor's antennae fully extended, the unforeseen happened. Management not only burst through that crack in the door, they broke the door down and trampled it. That door remains down. The upshot of which is that, even today, at companies that are otherwise healthy and profitable, the union still dreads seeing management's agenda. That's how radically the dynamic has shifted.

A comparison can be made to the way the Bush administration, following the attack of 9-11, used the specter of "terrorism" as an excuse for acts of foreign aggression and domestic civil liberties infringements. Once the opportunity presented itself, the administration played it for all it was worth. Corporate America did the same with the unions.

While it was the downturn in the auto industry that changed everything, not just for the UAW but for organized labor at large, it has to be acknowledged that, as the philosopher said, "perception is everything." And when President Reagan fired those 11,000 striking air traffic controllers, in 1981, what remained of labor's perceived invincibility was more or less wiped out.

Unions have been playing catch-up ever since. Needless to say, with the emergence of the global economy and the loss of America's manufacturing base, regaining their influence is going to be an uphill battle.

Still, with the labor vs. management dichotomy being as fundamental and deep-seated as it is, labor's revitalization is inevitable. One can argue that the groundwork for organized labor's resurgence is already in place. It's only a matter of time before the pendulum swings the other way.

CounterPunch
2008

HOW WAL-MART CAN BE BEATEN

Wal-Mart Stores, Inc. is not only the largest private-sector employer in the United States (with more than 3,600 stores and 1.2 million employees), it's the largest private-sector employer in both Mexico and Canada as well. It already has 60 stores in what is quaintly referred to as Communist China, with plans for more. As an example of the clout Wal-Mart wields, it was able to persuade Procter & Gamble to invent a whole new version of "Tide" detergent, one that would be more suitable for the manual wash-machines used in China.

Anyone who's seen Wal-Mart's widely circulated promotional video can't help but be struck by the company's numbing arrogance and ambition. The video shows jubilant Chinese workers ("associates") dressed in matching T-shirts, doing group calisthenics while chanting corporate slogans. (That annoying whirring sound in the background is Chairman Mao spinning in his grave.)

It goes without saying that Wal-Mart's entire U.S. operation is non-union. Indeed, the Wal-Mart empire has come to symbolize everything labor unions despise in a non-union enterprise: stinginess, intractability, invincibility. But give Wal-Mart its due credit. Somehow it has managed to convince a million unprotected, under-appreciated, under-paid and under-insured "associates" that labor unions and exploitation go together like vodka and regrets. That's no small feat.

In early 2003, the AFL-CIO launched a massive drive to organize Wal-Mart's U.S. operation. Besides devoting enormous time and money (reportedly, tens of millions of dollars) to the effort, the union unveiled its ambitious plan in a gaudy press release. Because Wal-Mart is to anti-collectivist sentiment what Babe Ruth was to baseball, cracking its enamel-like shell was a chance for Big Labor to show what it could do on center stage.

Instead, as most are aware, the AFL-CIO failed to organize a single store. Not one. With 3,600 ducks on the pond, and the world's most expensive shotgun in their lap, they couldn't hit a single duck. This shrieking failure was so disappointing, so staggering, that the House of Labor, to this day, has not fully recovered from it. In truth, the recent splintering of the AFL-CIO into a rival labor conglomerate called "Change to Win" was a direct consequence of the Wal-Mart debacle.

As for that splintering, a digression: Nothing against SEIU president Andrew Stern and his band of mutineers (they did what they felt had to be done), but doesn't "Change To Win" sound like something spawned at a management retreat? Change to Win. It has the smarmy, unmistakable ring of seminar-speak. Wouldn't something terse and hopeful, like the "New Alliance," or weirdly haunting, like "Ergo Nation," have been better?

In any event, the AFL-CIO's traditional game-plan for attracting new members is now considered too conservative, too genteel, to be effective. In a word, it's seen as obsolete. You won't convince workers as indoctrinated as Wal-Mart's to embrace a union simply by passing out handbills and solidarity buttons. A new approach is required.

Labor needs to drop a bomb. It needs to introduce to the Wal-Mart crowd the agitprop concept of class-warfare. Introduce the concept the way the early fur traders introduced rum to the Mohawks. Provoke these workers; arouse them, inflame them, goad them, dare them, shame them into taking action.

To transform these gentle retailers into "Wal-Martyrs," the union must resort to psychological hellfire and brimstone. These workers need to be insulted, not educated. Appeal to their American sense of fair play. Tell them the truth. Tell them that so long as Wal-Mart's executives regard them as weak-minded and gutless, they will continue to piss on them from a great height

Use psychodrama. Suggest that what we have here is high school all over again, and that the same dynamic that prevailed then prevails now. Use the class-warfare template: Workers are the "regular" kids—the majority, the decent, nose-to-the-grindstone core of the school. Wal-Mart executives are the rich, conceited students, spoiled kids who dress too well, whose parents buy them expensive cars and pay for abortions.

But unlike high school, where the choices were limited to envying, resenting or ignoring this privileged class, a labor union provides an additional choice. You can now defy them. You can overthrow them. You can pull the pompous bastards off the edifice and make them eat cafeteria food, just like the rest of us.

There's a memorable line in the movie, "The Usual Suspects": "The greatest trick Satan ever played was convincing the world he didn't exist." That same quote could apply to the concept of class-warfare. Somewhere along the way we began pretending that class distinctions don't exist. But they do exist. You can find them, along with everything else, at your neighborhood Wal-Mart.

CounterPunch
2008

DON'T BALK AT THE WORD "ADVERSARIAL"

The case can be made that, during the mid-1980s, America's labor unions made a critical and momentous error in judgement. Their error was to trust management, to buy into the corporate slogan declaring that labor relations were no longer "adversarial" in nature.   Their error was to buy into the corporate announcement that labor relations had turned a corner, and that those "bad old days" of head-butting and mutual acrimony were gone forever.

Arguably, the decline of organized labor can be partly traced to this watershed moment. It can be traced to the moment when unions were lured into believing the fairy-tale notion that working people—those earning an hourly wage and permanently relegated to the bottom of the food chain—were full-fledged members of what was now being euphemistically referred to as the "team."

In truth, hourly workers are (and have always been) regarded as little more than "overhead." To management, hourly workers are a necessary but regrettable business expense, a drag on company assets, an impediment to profit. To suggest that labor and management are "on the same team" is to engage in a perverse fantasy. It's a phrase that has all the earmarks of being spawned in one of those odious human resource seminars. Even the rank-and-file members smirked when they first heard it.

To fully appreciate what management *really* thinks of its workers, just consider the research and development money that has been spent on robotics. It amounts to billions of dollars. This infatuation with robots says everything we need to know about Corporate America's respect for the dignity and purposefulness of working people. Management's ultimate dream is to replace living, breathing human beings with "mechanical men." That says it all.

So it's not a coincidence that the moment management succeeded in convincing unions that "both sides want the same thing" happened to be the exact moment when corporate earnings began to soar, when CEO salaries began spiraling wildly upward, and when workers' wages and benefits began their precipitous slide downward, a decline that continues to this day. Union resistance was the last hurdle to clear; getting the unions to capitulate was the last jewel in the crown.

This observation is not intended as an indictment of organized labor. Rather, it's meant as a sad commentary on a sad set of circumstances. Moreover, even though the membership was skittish at any talk of a "partnership" with management, it's not meant to imply that had union leadership *not* bought into this rhetoric, things today would be different, because, clearly, that's not the case—at least not for the traditional "smoke-stack" unions. Far from it.

With the startling emergence of the global economy and the exploitation of cheap labor on the world market, the hollowing-out of America's manufacturing base was more or less inevitable. Because it was in this sector's core industries (steel, automobiles, paper, rubber, heavy equipment, etc.) that the attractive union jobs were found, when these industries were decimated, labor was crippled. Walter Reuther himself could have risen from the grave, and not been able to stop it.

But even if the decline of manufacturing was "inevitable," what didn't need to happen was the *surrender* of organized labor. What didn't need to happen was a decade's worth of give-backs, takeaways, and countless accommodations, indignities and instances of the union bending over backwards, few of which, ultimately, led to any long-term benefits.

After all, what was actually gained? Besides being congratulated by management for entering into a New Realm of labor relations, what tangible thing did unions gain by joining the "team"? Union membership continued to plummet. Workers continued to be laid off. Companies continued doing what they'd always done—i.e., maneuvered to maximize profits. Things continued to get worse. But wouldn't they have gotten worse even without labor's capitulation?

34

Consider: What would have happened if labor *hadn't* bought into the New Philosophy? What would have happened if unions had stuck with their "adversarial" approach and negotiated accordingly? What would have happened if, sensing a painful and demoralizing long-term future, unions went after all the short-term swag they could get?

While those questions can't be answered, one thing is clear: Labor unions were effectively co-opted. They were gamed. Despite labor's sincerity and willingness to play ball—to attend team-building seminars, extend or renegotiate existing contracts, embrace the Deming Philosophy, form "quality circles," et al—factories continued to shut down and jobs continued to be shipped out of the country.

Looking back on it, what labor's acquiescence did, more than anything, was grease the skids for management, make it easier for them. Getting the unions off their back must have seemed like a dream come true, something no one, not even the wildest optimist, would have thought possible in the 1970s. Being neutered is bad enough; being persuaded to do the snipping yourself is a whole other humiliation.

There's a term in management called "harvesting" a business. It applies to leaving a business in such a way as to maximize every last opportunity for making money on the way out.

For example, when a company shuts down a factory or one of the factory's main production lines, management rarely announces its plan in advance of what is required, by law, in accordance with the 1989 WARN Act (which requires 60 days notice of a plant shutdown or the layoff of 50 or more employees).

Even with rumors circulating to the contrary, management reassures everyone that a shutdown is unlikely. Telling workers that there's going to be a cutback or termination of a production line could negatively affect morale, which, in turn, could negatively affect production.

Therefore, in order to squeeze the maximum profit out of a dying enterprise, they do the opposite. They spread the word that, even though things are looking bad, if people work harder and if production increases significantly, the chances are good that the product line will be retained and everyone will keep their job. In this way they're able to "harvest" the enterprise.

In 1992, the Kimberly-Clark Corp. did this very thing with its infant care operation at the Fullerton, California, paper mill. Despite increased sales of their extremely popular "Huggie" disposable diaper, Kimberly-Clark continued to cut back on the number of machines producing them at their diaper plants, nation-wide.

Because machine speeds and efficiency had increased dramatically, 28 machines in the corporation were now producing what it took 42 machines to do just a year or so earlier. The increased productivity was spectacular. Machines that previously ran at 300 dpm (diapers per minute), were now purring along at speeds in excess of 500 dpm, and the rates were continuing to climb.

Having already seen 4 of its 6 machines shut down, the Fullerton diaper crews were understandably nervous. Even as Fullerton's production and efficiency numbers continued to increase, the writing on the wall was clear. As much as people tried to remain upbeat, seeing a huge, expansive diaper department with 2 lonely diaper machines in it was cause for worry. Because it wasn't a plant shutdown, and the total number employees was under 50, the company wasn't obligated to give notification.

Still, whenever company executives visited Fullerton and were asked outright by hourly workers or union officers if the diaper department had a future, they were assured that it had. They were told that, if the production rates continued to improve, "it's going to be awful hard to shut you guys down." Of course, this gave everyone hope.

The operation was shut down soon after the last visit. Ironically, the month the diaper plant shut down happened to be the same month it set an all-time, single-month production record. While closing the place had been a foregone conclusion, it was one that management felt it couldn't risk sharing with the crews. And let me add that Kimberly-Clark was a good company, an enlightened company. I'd match their employee relations with any company in America.

Unfortunately, this same underlying strategy of "harvest" applied to unions across the country. American management had no intention of joining in any mutually beneficial partnership with organized labor. God forbid. All they were interested in was getting the unions to back off, to become less aggressive in their negotiations, to "heel," like obedient dogs, until companies could figure out how best to maximize their profit in a rapidly changing world. They succeeded.

The lesson here for organized labor is a simple one: Stay united, stay focused, don't trust anything that comes out of management's mouth. And above all, don't let the corporation pretend that labor-management relations aren't adversarial, because they are. Indeed, now more than ever.

CounterPunch
2008

AFTERMATH

Even after a group of employees goes through the hassle of getting enough signatures (30% of the workers) to force an employer to submit to a NLRB-sanctioned union election, and even after they survive the company's comprehensive anti-union propaganda campaign (usually consisting of disinformation and veiled threats), and manage to win that election (with a simple majority), it's not guaranteed that these employees will get a union contract.

Unfortunately, in many instances, winning the right to form a union is only the first step. Despite federal law requiring the parties to engage in "good faith" bargaining, many companies simply don't know how to take yes for an answer. After using every trick in the book to dissuade their employees from joining a union (and failing in that effort), companies go to the bargaining table with the prime objective of thwarting the negotiation process.

Speaking of "tricks" used in anti-union propaganda campaigns, one of my favorites involved a west coast manufacturing company that was determined to go the extra mile in keeping the union out. During the interim (after getting the necessary signatures but prior to the actual vote), the company forced its employees to attend mandatory meetings where they were subjected to an anti-union movie which was advertised as being sanctioned by the NLRB.

What?! The NLRB sponsored propaganda that opposed the establishment of labor unions? Well, not exactly. At the end of the movie, in very small print, the audience was informed that the initials "NLRB" stood for an organization called the "National Labor Reference Bureau," and that this organization was not to be confused with the actual National Labor Relations Board.

But back to company strategy at the bargaining table. Management's chief tactic in these instances is simply to stall. Its goal is to break down the union's resolve, to drag out the bargain to the point where the membership begins to have second thoughts. Knowing that they have a freshly elected rookie negotiating team facing them, one sent there by an earnest but naive workforce looking to secure its very first contract, the company attempts to exploit that dynamic.

What they do is refuse to agree to the majority of the union's agenda. Besides coming in shamelessly low on the obvious cost items (wages and benefits), the company takes an intransigent position on standard, boilerplate language: they refuse to agree to the establishment of a standing committee to adjust grievances, refuse to include a binding arbitration clause, and refuse to agree to automatic dues withdrawals (where monthly dues are automatically taken out of the employees' paychecks, a practice done in the overwhelming majority of union shops), forcing union officers to collect dues themselves, an arduous, time-consuming process.

Another tactic is to refuse to agree to provisions and practices that are already in place, ones that have been observed for years, before the vote to make it a union shop. For example, the company will refuse to recognize a certain holiday as a day off with pay, even though it's been a common practice. The company's message: "You didn't trust management to take care of you. You wanted a union. Fine. Now see how hard it is to get a decent contract."

A newly formed union membership is vulnerable, particularly at their first negotiation. They've just voted to affiliate and, while excited and still a bit intimidated by the prospect, don't quite know what to expect. When the company plays hardball, refusing to sign anything that comes close to resembling a fair agreement, it puts enormous pressure on the employees. No one, not even the most vocal leaders of the organizing campaign, wants to go out on strike. After all, the whole point of forming a union was to improve their economic status, not to wind up hitting the bricks as a first step.

And then there are the dissenters, those members who voted against affiliation, who didn't want a union in the first place. The longer it takes for the company to agree to a contract, the more influence these people have on the floor. When things turn ugly at the bargaining table, it's not uncommon for a decertification drive to begin, often fueled by company gadflies. With what started out as an opportunity to better themselves via a union contract having turned into a bitter struggle, with rumors of a strike now in play, people begin second-guessing their decision to form a union.

Even with representatives from the parent International giving assistance at the bargain, it's very difficult keeping the troops focused when the company is purposely dragging it out. Typically, the International will file an unfair labor practice (ULP) charge with the NLRB, accusing the company of failing to negotiate in good faith, but this does little to change the situation. ULPs are seldom upheld; and, in any event, the investigation and appeal periods take too long to make them a viable weapon.

What happens more often than not in these situations is that the union either agrees to an inferior contract, or the company signs what is called an "implemented agreement." An implemented agreement is where the union refuses to sign a woefully inferior contract, but also, for whatever reasons, decides not to go on strike, leaving the company to "implement" the agreement (more or less signing the union's name to it).

In a few cases, the membership decides to decertify. The newly formed union members vote to abandon their union. Sometimes they choose to reaffiliate with another union (blaming the failure to get a decent contract on the International), sometimes they choose to remain unaffiliated, to go it alone. But in any event, it's a victory for the company.

So next time we read about a workforce winning a NLRB union vote, let's not assume they've "won" anything yet. If the company is a bad loser and intends to take the fight to the next level, the union has got its work cut out for them.

CounterPunch
2007

ALCOHOL AS METAPHOR

"I have taken more out of alcohol than alcohol has taken out of me."
—Winston Churchill

Some years ago, when I was a union rep with the West Coast papermakers, I was called in on a DOJ case (drunk on the job) to represent an employee who was facing termination. While DOJs were by no means common, they weren't exactly rare, either.

Alcohol cases vary dramatically in how they're perceived. If a professor or judge shows up drunk, it's amazing how sympathetic people can be. They become almost *maternal* in their concern. Someone this accomplished, this educated, doing something this *disgraceful* can mean only one thing: the man is "fighting personal demons." A drunken judge? Oh my god, there has to be some tragic human story to explain it.

But let it be a factory worker who's been drinking, and the guy is regarded as a low-class degenerate who needs to be fired immediately. But what about this man's "personal demons"? Screw his personal demons. He's fired. Get him the hell out of here.

The employee in question ("Fred") was a middle-aged man, with over twenty years of service, working the nightshift as an operator of a high-speed packaging machine. While not staggering, fall-down drunk, he was, despite his denials, obviously under the influence. He smelled of alcohol, his eyes were shot, and he was slurring his words.

Although a company can't force a blood test—and a refusal doesn't automatically mean you're guilty—a refusal will definitely hurt your chances in arbitration. Not surprisingly, Fred declined to take a blood test. But when they asked him if he'd been drinking, he candidly told them he'd had "a few beers" before leaving for work, but insisted he wasn't drunk. That confession, by itself, was grounds for discharge.

So they fired him. A security guard accompanied him to his locker to collect his gear, which they stuffed into a lawn bag, and the company called his wife to come pick him up. Fred and I and the company nurse (who'd been summoned by Human Resources) stood at the plant entrance, awaiting his ride. Not knowing what to say, the three of us barely spoke. Minutes went by without anyone saying a word.

When his wife arrived, Fred had already sobered up sufficiently to appreciate what had just happened, and when he climbed unsteadily into the passenger seat, he looked about as melancholy and godforsaken as any 56-year old unemployed man could look. It was a pitiful sight. This was 1988.

Union veterans have told me that during the 1960s and '70s, the company treated DOJs much differently. Although drinking was definitely frowned upon—not only by management, but by the union, as well—instead of being automatically fired, employees suspected of being intoxicated were often removed from the factory floor and sent home without incident.

Because the supervisors, technically, didn't have the authority to mitigate the punishment (i.e., issue a write-up or suspension in lieu of a discharge), but didn't want to see the guy lose his job, they simply got him out of there as quickly as they could and pretended it never happened.

While they usually called a family member to come get him, it wasn't unheard of to have an agreeable shop steward drive him home; and in some cases—if he lived close by or didn't appear too drunk—the guy was actually permitted to drive himself. Granted, letting him drive was a dumb move, but the gesture was indicative of the sensibilities that existed a generation ago.

By the time I got involved, everything had changed. The term "zero tolerance" was already on the horizon, and employees suspected of being under the influence were treated with a weird mixture of competing attitudes: utter revulsion and disgust mixed with the brusque, impersonal professionalism of a triage unit.

Consider the contrast: In 1971, the facility's plant manager was himself an alcoholic. Once, after a night of boozing, he challenged the president of the union to a fistfight in a local bar, and had to be restrained by subordinates. It was a famous incident, one that union officials still gleefully recount. Compare this with 1988, when the plant manager was an abstemious Christian fundamentalist who held regular prayer sessions in his office. True.

In alcohol cases, HR always used the same two arguments. First, they said a drunk man working around moving equipment was a safety hazard, not only to himself, but to his fellow employees (which was probably true). "We're firing him for *your* benefit, not *ours*," is what they liked to say.

And second, when the union requested that he be suspended and placed in rehab instead of fired (because crew safety, by their own admission, was their chief concern), they went Hobbesian on us. They argued that *suspending* rather than *firing* him would be an invitation to everyone in the facility to have one drunken incident "free of charge," without fear of losing their job, a conclusion so bizarre and cynical, only a certified HR creature could have come up with it.

No one is condoning drunkenness or denying that alcoholism is a serious and debilitating disease. No one is saying it's cool to drink on the job. The damage alcohol has done to individuals and families is a matter of record. I'm simply using alcohol as a metaphor, showing that drinking in the workplace has been treated differently in different contexts and in different eras, and suggesting that those differences speak to a larger issue.

A generation ago, most front-line supervisors were former hourly employees who'd been promoted into management, and most of their parents had been blue-collar workers. They were sympathetic to working people. This all changed in the 1980s, when front-line supervision was given over to young college grads who not only viewed workers as "factory apes," but whose parents were typically white-collar.

A generation ago, there was also a greater sense of *community*. While hourly and salaried workers obviously differed in their respective job skills and backgrounds, in a broader sense, they perceived themselves as being positioned on the same axis, as points along the same continuum.

Accordingly, top executives made salaries in the range of 15-20 times what the hourly workers made, not the 200-400 times it is today. Company executives in the 1970s were regarded as just that—well-compensated businessmen—not as corporate mandarins who flew in private jets and lived in gated mansions.

Corny as it sounds, these blue-collar folks and their bosses had a grudging respect for each other. Yes, they battled and bickered and embarrassed themselves, and yes, there were grievances and strikes; but they also genuinely *engaged* each other. There were joint union-management bowling leagues, softball games, company picnics, talent shows, and Christmas parties. Adversaries or not, there was a *connection*.

Most of that stuff was ancient history by the time I became a rep. Moreover, instead of being the adversaries of old, the company assured us that management and the union were now on the same team. "Why should we beat our heads against the wall, when we both want the *same* thing?" an HR director once asked me.

Of course, that was a lie; union and management didn't want the same thing. Working people wanted a larger slice of the pie, and the company wanted to give them a smaller slice. Pretending that both sides wanted the same thing was a cruel hoax. Predictably, once the union was embraced as "teammates," wages began slipping, benefits began declining, and work rules began stiffening.

What happened next was hideous. Loyal employees woke up one morning to find that not only had their standard of living been hollowed-out, but that they had been stripped of their dignity as workers. Instead of being proud union warriors, they were now palace eunuchs.

The castration had been a three-step process. Initially put in motion by the Taft-Hartley Act, way back in 1947, it was followed, sequentially, by policies of the Reagan and Clinton administrations, and culminated in the "team-building" philosophy of corporate HR. Since then, of course, everything has gotten worse.

The Exception Magazine

2009

STEVE FORBES ON THE WARPATH

> "All sin tends to be addictive, and the terminal point of addiction is what is called damnation."
> —W.H. Auden

One would have to be a dyed-in-the-wool Pollyanna or plain fool not to recognize that labor unions in this country, despite all the good they've done and continue to do, are fighting for their collective lives. Indeed, it requires every resource at labor's disposal just to keep their heads above water. Things are grim.

On one side, unions face a deadly, triple-threat combination—Corporate America looking to outsource everything that can be manufactured or digitalized; Joe Citizen buying into all the anti-labor propaganda he's being bombarded with; and Republican lawmakers seeking to further marginalize unions through the courts and government agencies.

Alternatively, on the other side, unions face their traditional allies and benefactors, the Democrats, who continue to embarrass themselves and disappoint the Movement by pretending to be organized labor's staunch supporter, yet rarely go out on a limb to help. Meanwhile, the once proud and healthy middle-class continues to be chipped away.

This is not to say the battle is over, or that, despite their woeful current predicament, unions aren't capable of making a dramatic comeback. In fact, given the climate of the country and the fundamental dichotomy and tension that has always existed between labor and management (in spite of those slick "We're all on the same team" slogans), it can be argued that labor's eventual resurgence, in one form or another, is almost guaranteed.

Still, just when it seemed that organized labor had been battered, slandered and beaten down about as much as it could be, we find that there's no end to it. New plots continue to be hatched, new enemies continue to be recruited.

For those wondering whatever happened to Steve Forbes, the one-time Republican presidential candidate and radical flat tax disciple, he has recently resurfaced as a shill for a virulently anti-union organization called the National Right to Work Legal Defense Foundation (NRTWLDF).

In a letter dated April 28, 2008, Forbes implored the readers on his mailing list to heed the dangers posed by America's labor unions, and urged them to fill out the enclosed questionnaire and mail it back immediately. His 4-page letter is filled with anti-union diatribe. Here's a sample:

> "Fueled by massive forced-dues dollars seized from employees as a condition of employment, union bosses are now on a legislative rampage to help the new far-left majority. Big Labor is pulling out all the stops to:
> - block the appointment of qualified judges on the nations' Federal courts;
> - further reduce parental control over their children's education and hand it to unaccountable teacher unions and government bureaucrats;
> - stop lawsuit and medical malpractice reform needed to restrain greedy trial lawyers;
> - retain the unfair federal "Death Tax" and cancel the Bush tax cuts; and
> - seize new powers to collect hundreds of millions of dollars in forced union dues."

The questionnaire (titled "Voter Opinion Survey on Big Labor") consists of nine questions, most of them emotionally loaded, categorical and wildly misleading.

Some examples:

> Question #1: "Do you think American workers should be fired for refusing to pay dues to a union?"
>
> Question #6: "Do you think union violence should continue to enjoy legal immunity under federal law and the laws of more than 15 states?"

Question #8: "Do you believe that public employees such as police and firefighters should be forced to join labor unions?"

Very weird stuff.

Instead of focusing their outrage and fury on the federal government—for wantonly violating the civil liberties of American citizens, spending billions of dollars a month on an unpopular war, propping up maggoty oligarchies all over the globe, and bailing out greedy Wall Street investors (not to mention engaging in perjury and every other manner of deception)—this NRTWLDF group feels compelled to go after working men and women.

Of course, these are the same folks who opposed the establishment of a mandatory federal minimum wage and the creation of OSHA (Occupational Health and Safety Administration), and who favor privatizing social security. By and large, they're the same closet-plutocrats who claim to "respect" working people but try to conceal the fact that the average American worker hasn't received an *actual* (allowing for cost of living) wage increase since 1973.

Because these anti-union zealots can't come out and honestly say what they really feel—i.e., that the notion of common working people getting a substantially larger slice of the pie makes them ill—they attack the organizations representing these workers. They use lurid, smear tactics in their attack, depicting labor unions as corrupt, dictatorial and greedy. The following paragraph is taken from the second page of Forbes' letter:

> "For America's workers, it's not much of a choice. Either pay tribute to labor chieftains or lose their jobs. But for union bosses, it's like cashing in a giant lottery jackpot every day of the year. And their lust for money is nearly endless."

If the ideology being peddled here weren't so scary and potentially dangerous, that paragraph would be funny . . . funny

48

in the same way the movie "Reefer Madness" was funny. Unfortunately, the stakes are too high to appreciate the humor.

It's hard to understand why class distinctions remain so powerful in America. People don't flinch when they hear of a hedge fund manager, like John Paulus, who made $2.5 *billion* in 2007 via the quasi-legal manipulation of money, yet they get downright resentful when they hear of a group of janitors asking to be paid $14/hour ($29,000 annually). It's hard to understand. And it ain't fair.

CounterPunch
2008

THE CHRYSLER-UAW DEAL

May 2, marked the third anniversary of the death of Harry Bernstein (who died in 2006, at age 83), the celebrated labor writer for the Los Angeles Times. The Times hired Bernstein in 1962 to write a weekly column about labor union issues, the first such column in the pro-business newspaper's long history. The column ran, in the Business section, all the way until 1993.

Anyone who followed Harry's career, and came to respect his eccentric but egalitarian pro-union slant, has to wonder what he would have thought of Chrysler's Chapter 11 and the UAW's soon-to-be substantial stake in the company.

Given how much of a "workplace democracy" booster Harry was (he was one of the first labor writers to promote the philosophy of Dr. Edwards Deming), it's fair to surmise he would've welcomed it—albeit with a healthy list of qualifications.

I first encountered Harry in the summer of 1983, when, out of the blue, he phoned our AWPPW union hall, asking for details on the strike we had just called against the Kimberly-Clark Corporation. With the hall in a state of near chaos, and no one officially assigned to man the desk or deal with the media, I just happened to be the person who picked up the telephone.

Things were incredibly tense. Because the strike came as a surprise (it was the first shutdown in 20 years), the union hall was filling up with people who wanted to know what was going on, how long the strike would last, when strike benefits would kick in, how much the benefits would be, plus a hundred other questions. Without air-conditioning, in the middle of July in Southern California—and with, literally, a hundred people crammed into it—this low-slung, cramped room was like bad real estate in Hell.

We'd been on the bricks, officially, for all of four hours (we shut down at noon, and it was now 4:00 PM), and yet the LA Times had already gotten the story and was sniffing around for more. For reasons that I admit were totally irrational, the notion of a newspaper reporter aggressively invading our privacy, looking for an angle, infuriated me. I accused him of having the same morbid fascination with our shutdown that sicko people had with gory traffic accidents.

Harry calmly replied that the labor beat was the way he made his living, and that he was simply trying to gather more information. In his gentlemanly, North Carolina drawl, he respectfully suggested that if I was unable to handle the pressure, I might consider passing the baton to someone else (ouch).

I abruptly ended the discussion by rattling off the reasons we had called the strike (I'd been sitting at the negotiating table for four months and knew them by heart), and invited him to call back later in the week, which he did. Despite this rocky start, we sort of became friends, and talked regularly over the next several years.

One of Harry's sage (and often repeated) observations was that unions must distinguish between what they *want* and what they *need*. Instead of looking for bosses who were wildly generous or enlightened or forgiving or easily intimidated, etc., labor unions should, instead, be looking for bosses who were *smart*—smart enough to keep the company afloat—because the one thing unions needed more than anything else was a reliable place to work.

Yes, a union is going to battle management over wages, benefits and working conditions—and Harry heartily approved of that militancy because he knew it was the only way workers could get what's coming to them—but for that battle to be sustainable, they have to have a healthy enterprise.

Corporate hubris and arrogance were his favorite targets. It angered and frustrated him that management didn't trust their own workers enough to tap into their on-the-job expertise. This Chrysler (and General Motors) debacle is a good example of that.

Already the long-knives are out, with everyone blaming everyone else for this Chrysler mess. Business groups are blaming the union for having been too greedy, and the union is blaming management for poor planning and demonstrating an almost criminal case of myopia. Although critics of the UAW are trying to make $28 per hour sound like a princely wage, when's the last time you gushed when someone walked in the room and boasted of making $56, 000 a year?

More to the point, those decent, $28 per hour jobs are dinosaurs. The current entry rate at a UAW plant is $14 per hour. That part of the American Dream—where the country's factory workers were allowed to belong to the middle-class—is more or less over.

Not only has the UAW made extraordinary concessions in wages and benefits, but America's manufacturing sector has had to listen for decades to insulting accusations that we can't compete with foreigners because, alas, Americans simply "aren't good enough workers." We're too spoiled.

Of course, that myth of the "spoiled American worker" has been utterly destroyed by the fact that Toyota, Nissan, Honda, Mercedes, BMW, Volvo, Hyundai, and Kia are rapidly building manufacturing plants all over the American South, and getting huge subsidies from those state governments to do it.

If Toyota honestly believed the American worker couldn't assemble a decent car, they wouldn't have built several plants in this country. In truth, what these foreign companies most love about Dixie (besides the billions of dollars in subsides) is the low wages, the lax pollution standards, and the anti-union bias. Sort of reminiscent of what the U.S. likes about the Third World, no?

The way this Chrysler arrangement is structured, the UAW's massive VEBA (Voluntary Employee Beneficiary Association) fund will control 55-percent of the equity in the company once it clears bankruptcy. In addition to a majority share of the company, the UAW will be given a seat on the Chrysler board of directors.

52

While this is being hyped as a bold and dramatic move, it can also be argued that it's largely a symbolic gesture. After all, what will having one seat and one vote really matter? Granted, as a board member, you'll be able to examine the books close up, just like the rest of the boys, but beyond that you'll be all but ignored.

In 1980, a big deal was made of giving Douglas Fraser, then president of the UAW, a seat on Chrysler's board of directors. Big deal or not, nothing much came of it. Even though Fraser was a bona fide board member, he was still a lone voice in the wilderness. The measures passed the board by a vote of 19 to 1. ("Thanks for your input, Doug.")

For this Chrysler partnership to pan out, the automaker needs to be successful, because owning 55-percent of a failed enterprise is suspiciously close to owning 55-percent of nothing. And even with the Fiat merger (and Fiat's CEO's brilliant track record), there is great cause for concern, as Chrysler's sales in April dropped a precipitous 48-percent. Clearly, they'll be digging themselves out of a deep hole, with the union clinging to their backs.

Still, even with all the negatives, uncertainties and platitudes— and despite the UAW being called "sellouts" and "dupes"—the union had no choice but to go for this deal. Their members' pensions are protected by the Treasury Department, and their retiree medical benefits are well-funded. It was a calculated move.

Was this Chrysler arrangement something the UAW hoped for? Absolutely not. Never. Would they have predicted, in their wildest dreams, that something like this could ever happen? Again, no. But it's the hand they were dealt, and they're playing it the smartest way they know how.

CounterPunch
2009

UNION ASSAULT: THE KENTUCKY RIVER DECISION

> "People of the same trade seldom meet together,
> even for merriment and diversion, but the
> conversation ends in a conspiracy against the
> public, or in some contrivance to raise prices."
> —Adam Smith, The Wealth of Nations

There are two "wars" going on in this country, each of which has the power to dramatically affect the future of working people. One is the war being waged by organized labor, seeking (through membership drives, lobbying and political contributions) to expand its base, gain new members, and galvanize its existing membership against assaults from anti-union forces.

This war to "recruit and maintain" is an uphill battle. The AFL-CIO's recent failure to organize even *one* of Wal-Mart's then 3,600 stores in the U.S. (today there are 4,000), despite allocating enormous resources to the effort, is an indication of just how daunting a mission this is.

The other war is a political one. It is a war being waged by the Bush administration's Department of Labor, Department of Justice and National Labor Relations Board (NLRB), a war committed to reducing even further labor's diminishing influence.

The corporation-owned Bushies have a clear mandate: To cripple organized labor. And they've been busy at it, being creative. For example, the administration has attempted to strip the collective bargaining privileges from the 160,000 employees of the Department of Homeland Security, and has argued that graduate assistants and temp workers cannot, by law, seek union representation. They've been busy.

But one of the most significant recent battles in this war was the October, 2006, ruling by the Bush-appointed NLRB, involving three separate groups of health care employees. It has come to be known collectively as the "Kentucky River" decision.

A bit of history: While the 1935 National Labor Relations Act (the "Wagner Act") gave unions the statutory right to organize workers and to act as their sole representative in the collective bargaining process, the anti-union 1947 Taft-Hartley Act added a key restriction. Taft-Hartley stipulated that "supervisory personnel" were exempt from the statute. In short, managers, supervisors and other "bosses" were not allowed to be represented by a union. No supervisors allowed. Fair enough.

To clarify the restriction, the Taft-Hartley Act defined a supervisor as:

> ". . . any individual having authority, in the interest of the employer, to hire, transfer, suspend, lay off, recall, promote, discharge, assign, reward, or discipline other employees, or responsibly to direct them, or to adjust their grievances, or effectively to recommend such action, if in connection with the foregoing the exercise of such authority is not of a merely routine or clerical nature, but requires the use of independent judgment."

The employees involved in the Kentucky River cases are nurses employed at nursing facilities in Kentucky—specifically "charge nurses," the ones who act more or less as lead persons, directing other nurses as to what patients need attending, what medications are to be administered, when to administer them, etc. Charge nurses have no managerial authority; they can't hire, fire, reprimand, reward, alter seniority or adjust the pay of their fellow workers.

Even though it's clear that the Taft-Hartley Act was not intended to apply to lead men, hourly clerical administrators or "straw bosses," the Bush administration's minions on the NLRB willfully misinterpreted its language, and ruled that charge nurses (while having no supervisory authority) fell into the broad category of "supervisor," and, therefore, did not qualify as employees eligible to join a union.

While this ruling was directed specifically against employees in a Kentucky nursing home, it's a decision (a "clarification") that has broad implications and clearly transcends the health care industry. Judging by the Bush administration's aggressive track record, nurses are just the first step.

Lame duck president or not, there's still time for this crew to severely damage the movement. The Kentucky River decision cuts to the heart of a worker's right to seek union representation, and affects, potentially, millions of employees across the United States.

In truth, the only way organized labor can hope to alter these and similar decisions is by electing a Democrat to the White House and having a *substantial* majority (not the razor thin one that exists now) of Democrats in the House of Representatives and Senate. There are simply too many enemies of labor lurking about—from corporations, libertarians, lobbyists, Republicans, the Supreme Court—to win this war by any other means.

Labor needs to regain, at least nominally, the control of the three political arms of the government. A Democrat—whether it's Clinton or Obama—can be depended upon to appoint an NLRB 5-person board that is infinitely friendlier to labor than the one that's been in place for the last seven years.

Only with a labor-friendly congress and a pro-labor president in the White House will it be possible for substantive changes to be made. As much as labor unions feel that they've been betrayed and let down by the Democrats (and, God help us, they have), they can't go it alone. There are simply too many obstacles in the way. They'll need help.

CounterPunch
2008

LABOR AND THE COURTS

Many will recall the ILWU (International Longshore and Warehouse Union) lockout of 2002, which shut down the west coast ports for 10 days and idled approximately 10,500 union workers, before President Bush invoked the Taft-Hartley Act and forced the parties back to the table.

Even for the relatively short time the docks were shut down, given the enormous volume of cargo the west coast handles (tens of thousands of tons a day), there were hundreds of ships stacked up for miles out into the Pacific Ocean, with hundreds more still moored at home ports around the globe awaiting word as to when the docks would reopen—all dressed up with no place to go.

Of course, during all this, the PMA (Pacific Maritime Association), the business organization that represents the shipping companies and terminal operators, was having a spaz attack. Millions of dollars an hour were being lost. The parties eventually settled their dispute and the ILWU proudly walked away with what was characterized by independent observers as a "victory for labor."

The ILWU and PMA are currently locked into another round of contract negotiations. And even though the union's contract has long since expired and both parties have complained publicly about the lack of movement from the other side, no one believes that another strike or lockout is imminent. The precarious state of the nation's economy, plus the fact that the union and PMA have already settled the health care issue, more or less precludes a strike as an option.

Still, recalling Bush's injunction, in 2002, it's interesting to note the government's role in labor relations. While it's accurate to say that the U.S. government, once upon a time, supported and assisted organized labor, it's also accurate to say that, for the last 60 years or so (certainly going back to the passage of the Taft-Hartley Act in 1947) the government and courts have systematically sought to thwart if not undermine the labor movement. Indeed, to that hackneyed question of What have you done for me lately? the government's answer to labor would be "Nothing. Absolutely nothing."

Okay, maybe "nothing" is too strong a verdict. Because there have been a few half-hearted attempts to assist labor, perhaps "precious little" would be the more accurate description. For example, in regard to the ILWU itself, it's been the pro-labor Democrats in congress who have successfully held off several attempts to remove the Longshoremen from the jurisdiction of the National Labor Relations Act (also known as the Wagner Act) and place them under the auspices of the Railway Labor Act, a move that would essentially prohibit the dockworkers from going on strike.

But, in truth, since the end of World War II, on those occasions when labor hasn't been pointedly ignored by the government, it's been harassed and attacked by it. Taft-Hartley, right to work laws, prohibitions against strikes, rulings against labor PACs, the Landrum-Griffin Act (1959), and a multitude of missed opportunities where the NLRB failed to uphold workers' rights—these have all combined to put unions in the position they find themselves. The grim truth is that it's not only American corporations who fear a strong, organized labor force, it's the U.S. government as well.

It's been said that the passage, in 1935, of the Wagner Act was, for labor, analogous to what the Declaration of Independence was for the colonies. Although unions had been flourishing (growing in size and influence, negotiating contracts) for a full century before the New Deal, it was Wagner that energized, stimulated and, most importantly, *legitimized* the labor movement.

However, even though the Wagner Act gets all the credit and glory for launching the modern labor movement, it was, arguably, the lesser known Norris-La Guardia Act, passed three years earlier (1932), that truly "liberated" the unions. Named for its congressional sponsors—Nebraska Senator George Norris and New York Representative Fiorello La Guardia—the Act was important for two reasons.

First, Norris-La Guardia made it illegal for employers to use so-called "yellow dog" contracts (where companies hired new employees only after they agreed, in writing, never to join a union); and, second, it drastically limited the authority of federal courts to prevent strikes by issuing blanket injunctions against them.

Prior to the Norris-La Guardia Act, pro-business judges were notorious for cutting the legs off union members by taking away their right to strike, using the old "general welfare of the public" as their catch-all grounds for forcing the rank-and-file back to work. Strikes are tough enough to use as leverage against management, even with a level playing field; but when a judge can step in on behalf of the business community and arbitrarily end one, labor doesn't stand a chance.

Injunctions are tricky propositions. Knowing when to step in can't be easy. While the courts have an obligation to protect citizens from undue hardship, when is a strike a genuine "threat" to the welfare of public, and when is it merely a monumental inconvenience?

Obviously, the loss of revenue to a business or industry can't be the determining factor, even if that loss is staggering. After all, inflicting financial punishment on the bosses via economic self-sacrifice by the workers is the whole point, isn't it? Take that right away, and you're left with nothing.

CounterPunch
2008

THE CALCULUS OF STRIKES

"Labor cannot, on any terms, surrender the right to strike."
—Louis Brandeis, Supreme Court Justice

An imperfect analogy: Strikes are to labor unions what stiff fines and the threat of a prison sentence are to the IRS— something that is seldom used, but whose presence is vital to maintaining credibility.

Although most union officials are aware that by-laws can vary widely from union to union (even from local to local, within the same union), for nearly 40 years the executive board of Local 672 of the AWPPW (Association of Western Pulp and Paper Workers) believed they were *compelled* by federal labor law to conduct their strike votes via secret ballot.

It made sense. Not only had they always done it that way, voting *secretly* on something as important as whether or not to give the negotiating committee strike authorization seemed like the only reasonable way to do it. A simple majority of the membership was required for approval (versus, for example, SAG by-laws, which require a 75% mandate).

As it turns out, a union may conduct a strike vote by various methods: secret ballot, a show of hands, even by acclimation (voice vote). Federal law is silent on the matter. And in the case of voting by acclimation, it's only when the differential between the "yeas" and "nays" isn't discernible that you're required to call for a show of hands. Other than that, you're free to pick your poison.

These same choices also apply to ratifying a contract, which also came as a surprise to local leadership. At Local 672, upon the conclusion of every contract negotiation, the membership was given a lengthy summary of the company's final offer, after which they were asked to enter polling booths, close the curtains, and vote for or against the new contract. It was wildly democratic. It was private. It made sense. And we'd always done it that way.

Moreover, the membership was so conditioned to ratifying a contract in the privacy of a shrouded booth, people would have freaked out if they'd been asked to do otherwise. If they'd been told to vote publicly—right there, out in the open, on the floor of the union hall—there would have been a raucous demonstration, if not a minor riot.

For the record, the only instances where secret balloting is *required* by federal labor law is in the election of officers and in matters involving money—e.g., raising the price of monthly union dues or initiation fees. So, while strike authorization and contract ratification can be done publicly (with all the attendant peer pressure and gawking that go along with it), when it comes to money, the members must be allowed to vote by secret ballot. It's a reasonable law.

Strikes themselves, although necessary, are traumatic, frightening undertakings. And, weirdly, they are virtually all alike. Despite significant differences between various industries and the unions affiliated with them, the cycle of emotions experienced by rank-and-file members during a strike is more or less identical. The arc consists of four distinct phases: euphoria, somber resolve, serious doubt, despair.

When you take a membership out on strike, you also have to realize that it's going to be tough getting them to seriously consider going out a second time, especially if memories are fresh, and the strike was a particularly difficult one. In fact, sometimes you can't even get a membership to give you strike authorization next time around, not if they think a walkout is a realistic possibility.

And who can blame them? A strike is a brutal thing, a case of self-inflicted economic homicide. Just because it is, undeniably, the only *real* (rather than *frivolous*) weapon a union brings to the bargaining table doesn't make it any easier getting through one.

Figuring out how to call a strike in such a way that it satisfies two key requirements—i.e., getting the company's attention and, at the same time, not spooking or financially crippling the membership—is how the notion of a "tactical" or "rolling" strike first took shape.

One of the problems with traditional strikes is that once you take the momentous step of pulling the plug, you never know how long you're going to be out of work. Even if your reasons for shutting down were eminently sound, and even if your membership was prepared for it, given the unpredictability of the company's response, you can never know the immediate outcome. You could be out three weeks or three months.

Also, if you go on strike for a particular purpose, it only makes sense that you stay out until you've achieved that purpose, otherwise the whole thing comes off looking like a monumental waste of time and money. But what if there's a standoff? What if management is as stubbornly locked into its position as the union committee is locked into theirs? Prolonged stand-offs can lead to *sieges*, rather than mere strikes, and sieges can massacre a union.

That's where the idea of the rolling strike comes in. In a rolling strike the union goes ahead and gives its 10-day notice to terminate the existing contract (such notification is required by law), exactly as it would at the outset of a "regular" strike. But in addition to announcing that the employees will be shutting down the operation at, say, one minute after midnight on such-and-such a date, the union also announces that they will be *returning* to their jobs at, say, 7:00 am, on such-and-such a date, five days later.

In short, a rolling strike is not open-ended; it has a clear and pre-determined life-span. This type of industrial action fulfills two objectives: You do the unthinkable, you shut down the company, you damage its ability to make a profit off your labor; but you also severely limit what that damage will be—both to the company's productivity and to the membership's pocketbooks.

An example of a tactical strike was the one recently called (on July 14) by service workers affiliated with AFSCME (American Federation of State, County and Municipal Employees) against the University of California, in which AFSCME members stayed out for five days before returning to work.

The danger in these things is that there's no guarantee the company will let you come back to work when you're finished. Because your 10-day notice has expired, technically, you have no contractual agreement with them; and with the contract terminated, there is no governing language prohibiting the company from locking you out.

This doesn't mean they *will* lock you out, only that it's *legal* for them to do so. While some companies are happy to get everyone back to work after a rolling strike, with no lingering hard feelings (as was the case, apparently, with the University of California and AFSCME), other companies may see it differently.

Other companies may view your little mini-mutiny as a form of treason and decide that their rebellious and "ungrateful" employees need to be taught a lesson. So you walk out all sassy and confident, with the intent of returning five days later, armed with increased leverage, and the company surprises you by keeping you out for two months. That's a textbook case of how a tactical strike blows up in your face.

Without question, the best strikes are the classic ones—the ones where you catch the company off-guard, where the membership is totally committed to the action, and where the shutdown results in tangible improvements in the areas you were going for. There used to be lots of those strikes, going back not only to the 1930s, but well before that.

Today, unfortunately, unless you're the ILWU (International Longshore and Warehouse Union), strikes have become far less effective. Still, until something better comes along, strikes are labor's only weapon. And, in truth, tough as things are, we need more of them, not less.

CounterPunch
2008

WAL-MART IS CAUGHT STEALING

Despite all the conjecture and second-guessing, there's no way to be certain that Iraq and Afghanistan would have turned out much differently had U.S. intelligence been more accurate, had Congress been given more information, had the media been more aggressive, or had Al Gore, instead of George Bush, been seated in the White House on that fateful day in September. We assume it would, but we can't be certain.

The same can be said of the Wall Street debacle. We can speculate all we like as to what might have happened had more "smart" people been doing their jobs and paying attention to the Big Picture, but there's no way to know for certain what, if anything, would have been done differently to prevent the catastrophe.

History has shown that people in positions of authority—whether in politics or commerce—don't always act on the evidence. Sometimes they postpone acting until it's too late; sometimes they succumb to popular opinion; sometimes they dispute or overrule or nit-pick or simply ignore the so-called "evidence." It happens.

But there's one thing we can be *absolutely* certain of. Had the employees of Wal-Mart been represented by a labor union, the company wouldn't be forced to pay $640 million in back wages to employees who were cheated out of that money. It never would have happened. Period.

Things in the workplace fall through the cracks all the time; they get dismissed, put off, overlooked, rescheduled, piled up, mishandled, etc.. But in a union shop, no one—and that means *no one*—fails to get paid. You can ask union people to work harder, to work safer, to work quicker; you can ask them pretty much anything, and they'll do it. Just don't ask them to work for free.

Predictably, even though Wal-Mart clearly got caught with its hand in the cookie jar (the settlement was the result of 63 class-action lawsuits), the company has tried to put a happy face on it, claiming that the whole thing was rather "complicated," and that the incidents in question occurred "a long time ago" and are in no way indicative what the company stands for today.

An employer trying to cut corners by cheating workers out of their pay isn't really that "complicated" a concept to grasp. It's pretty basic, actually. Moreover, it's a form of what is commonly known as "theft." And Wal-Mart did it knowingly and for the basest of reasons: they wanted to save money, and thought they could do it without getting caught. But they got caught. That's why they're paying $640 million.

Of course, the biggest shocker in all this is the fact that, despite Wal-Mart's history of stinginess and deceit, the company's employees are still independent. The world's largest retailer, with over 1.4 million employees, remains immaculately non-union (at least in the U.S.). Given that labor unions, across-the-board, offer superior wages, benefits, and working conditions, that circumstance is absolutely astonishing. Over 4,000 stores in the U.S., and not one of them is unionized? That is mind-boggling.

It's also a source of tension. In truth, the AFL-CIO is split on how to regard Wal-Mart's workforce, whom they've tried unsuccessfully to recruit for decades. To some union leaders, Wal-Mart employees are still seen as sorry, over-burdened and underpaid folks, too intimidated and frightened to go about joining a labor union, and condemned to suffer as a consequence.

Other union leaders take a less generous view. After years of futile organizing drives, they've come to regard Wal-Marters as ignoramuses and faux-individualists. They see them as stubborn, gullible and vain—a bunch of company lackeys who deserve every crappy thing that happens to them. If these people want the benefits of a union contract, then let 'em grow a pair, and join a union. Short of that, who gives a rat's ass what happens to them? Harsh as it sounds, that's how they see it.

After all, look at the facts. If a company spends millions of dollars trying to keep the union out, and preaches to its employees that unions are bad—that they're unnecessary, that they're a hindrance, that a union wouldn't help them—and then turns around and steals wages from the very people who are loyal to that company and who can barely make a living on the wages they're *already being paid,* what does that tell us?

Corporations cheat all the time. They cheat the competition by engaging in illegal or unethical business practices, they cheat the public through false advertising and poor quality, and they cheat Uncle Sam by not paying their fair share of taxes. The public has become inured to it.

But when a corporation steals from its own people—especially ones as fiercely loyal as Wal-Mart employees—doesn't that cross the line? Doesn't that totally blow their minds? What's it going to take for these gullible Wal-Marters to realize they're being exploited??

CounterPunch
2009

THE UAW JUNGLED-UP WITH GM MANAGEMENT

Anyone who's still curious about how American management *truly* feels about its hourly workforce need only reflect on the fact that billions of dollars a year are being spent on robotics technology. Indeed, robotics is one of the fastest growing industries in the world.

That's a sobering observation. When the bosses make it clear that they'd rather have mechanical men rather than real people doing the work, it doesn't bode well for the flesh-and-blood crowd. It's like a man confessing to a woman that, while he still loves and respects her, he prefers the inflatable doll.

So now we have General Motors, once the world's most conspicuous and prestigious symbol of capitalism, coming out of a Chapter 11 bankruptcy with the federal government owning 60% of it. Thirty years ago, you couldn't have made up this story; it would've been too preposterous, even as fantasy.

What this all means is that the United Auto Workers (UAW), the noblest and most revered union of them all—and the long-time adversary of both GM management and the federal government's labor laws—will now have two bosses: General Motors and the Federal Government. Incredible.

Naturally, all three sides—the company, the government, and the union—have gone on record saying that this was the last thing they wanted to see happen, that it was done, ultimately, out of a sense of urgency and desperation ("desperation" was the exact word Ron Gettlefinger, UAW's haggard president, used to describe it in his PBS interview).

But everybody needed this deal. GM needed it to survive as a company, the UAW needed it to survive as a union, and the government needed it avoid exacerbating an already serious recession. Had GM declared Chapter 7 (instead of Chapter 11), it would have meant liquidating the company and selling off its assets for pennies on the dollar.

More importantly (at least from the government's point of view), a Chapter 7 would have meant throwing tens of thousands of people out of work. Sixty thousand people losing their jobs (with an average annual income of, say, $50,000) would represent a loss to the economy of $3 billion—*per year.*

If it were just the bride's father who was armed, the GM restructure could be interpreted as your classic shotgun wedding. But in this instance, the bride, the groom, the bridesmaids, and both sets of in-laws were all toting shotguns. It would have been a blood-bath.

Some interesting features and implications of the Fall:

- It was the world's biggest industrial bankruptcy; and, with that $50 billion, GM became the second largest recipient of a federal bailout in history (AIG is first).

- Even if things go as hoped, and the company becomes profitable, the UAW will lose another 20,000 GM workers, going from 60,000 to an expected 40,000.

- General Motors had led the world market in car and truck sales for 76 consecutive years. In 2008, Toyota Motors finally replaced them as the leader. GM's U.S. market share has sunk to less than 20%.

- Instead of going outside the company to find a replacement for Rick Wagnoner (GM's former CEO and the man who green-lighted production of the Hummer), the new boss will be Fritz Henderson, GM's former COO (Chief Operating Officer).

- GM announced that $1,500 of the price of every new vehicle sold goes to paying employee health insurance.

- The South sees this as the greatest opportunity since Reconstruction. Foreign automakers are already pouring into Dixie, looking to take advantage of the low cost of living, lax pollution standards, and vehement anti-union bias. The

South views Detroit's troubles the way Ronald Reagan viewed the Berlin Wall coming down.

While no one can predict how this whole deal will work out, one thing is absolutely certain: without public support and consumer confidence, it will fail. If Americans don't start buying GM cars (not to mention Chryslers and Fords), the entire enterprise becomes academic, and Detroit is as good as dead.

People can debate all they like whether Detroit's collapse would be a "good" thing or "bad" thing, but there's no debating that it's a definite possibility. The country could find itself watching the hideous, agonizing death throes of a once-noble beast.

The Exception Magazine
2009

WHY AMERICA NEEDS LABOR UNIONS

"The only effective answer to organized greed is organized labor."

—Thomas Donahue

Labor is in the news again. As Detroit's multi-millionaire executives continue to mix it up with the struggling UAW, arguing over how to resuscitate a dying and woefully mis-managed industry without totally annihilating the wages and benefits the union spent 60 years fighting to get, the Obama administration agonizes over what to do next.

Of the Big Three automakers (Ford, General Motors and Chrysler) GM seems to be in the worst shape. In fact, on Feb. 14, it was leaked that GM plans to announce this week that unless it receives more federal loan guarantees (in addition to the $13 billion it already received), it will declare bankruptcy.

When the conversation turns to the topic of unions, it's discouraging to hear people praise organized labor's historical role in reshaping American society—more or less "inventing" the middle-class—and then, in the same breath, declare that unions are, at best, anachronisms, or, at worst, unwieldy obstacles to economic progress.

Many of the same folks who glowingly acknowledge labor's contributions—equal pay for women, abolishing child labor, the 8-hour day, the 5-day week, overtime premiums, paid vacation, sick pay, pensions, maternity leave, mandatory safety programs, and company-paid health insurance—will sigh and announce that, alas, we don't really need unions any more.

Presumably, because we now have all those goodies, they're unable to think their way to the next level. And that next level yields two truths: (1) Relations between Labor (those who work) and Management (those who pay for work) will always be adversarial; and (2) because Management possesses the lion's share of the wealth, resources, power, education, prestige and government patronage, Labor's only hope lies in organizing.

With the post-New Deal federal government having demonstrated that it is slavishly accommodating to Corporate America (despite the occasional crumb thrown labor's way), it should be apparent even to those who are uncomfortable with "collectivism" that the only entity capable of taking on Big Business is Big Labor. The choice for working people is either accepting "genteel poverty," or joining together and rising up.

Corporations are predictable. They hate paying taxes; they hate paying wages (the U.S. Chamber of Commerce has spent millions lobbying against raising the minimum wage, which, even today, at $6.55, is pitifully low); they hate unions; and they more or less hate the federal government, which they view as an impediment—until they need bailouts or regulations to stifle their competitors.

Kevin Phillips, former Republican strategist and speech writer for Richard Nixon, and author of the book, "The Politics of Rich and Poor," is no friend of labor. Far from it. But Phillips believes that citizens should be given the opportunity to prosper; and having watched in disbelief and disgust what happened during Ronald Reagan's two terms as president, he's afraid that, unless something reverses the trend, the phenomenon known as Middle-Class America will vanish forever.

What alarms Phillips is not only the "financialization" of the economy (the move away from manufacturing and into the credit industry), but the staggering gap that has developed between the wealthy and those in the middle and at the bottom. The rich are not only getting richer, they're manipulating the means by which they continue to broaden that gap.

Which brings us back to unions. As Phillips notes, the average worker's income hasn't risen in real dollars (taking into account cost of living) since 1973. Two incomes are now required to support a standard of living previously supplied by one. Polls show that while only 12.4 % of the workforce is organized, close to 60% of America's workers say they'd be interested in joining a union.

But why the discrepancy? Why only 12.4 % membership when so many more would like to join? While the abandonment of the manufacturing sector has, undoubtedly, resulted in the loss of many union jobs, Big Business is largely to blame for it. In collusion with Republicans and gutless Democrats, corporations—through stalling and intimidation tactics—have made it extremely difficult for workers to unionize.

Again, corporations are, by nature, neither altruistic nor generous. They are acquisitive. They are selfish. They are predatory. Corporations resent anything that stands in the way of making money, which is why they regard taxes as "robbery," and wages and benefits not as an investment in the workforce, but as "overhead."

And because union wages and benefits are roughly 15-20 % higher than non-union wages and bennies, Corporate America dreads labor unions and does everything in its power to neutralize them. Meanwhile, that staggering gap between the rich and the rest of us continues to grow. Even hardcore Republicans are alarmed by it.

Given the direction of the country, shouldn't labor unions be seen not only as *relevant*, but as absolutely *vital?* Without the unions propping up wages and benefits, who would do it? Arguably, without unions, the U.S. would become a glorified post-industrial oligarchy.

CounterPunch
2009

THREE REASONS FOR THE DECLINE OF UNIONS

"I wish I had a cause, because I have a lot of enthusiasm."
—Mort Sahl

Going from a high-water mark of 35% (in the 1950s) to the measly 12% it is today, national union membership has clearly taken a righteous beating. Lots of reasons, not least of which is passage of the Taft-Hartley Act (1947), which, with its comprehensive restrictions on union activities, has proven to be a genuine impediment to the labor movement.

Taft-Hartley aside, here are three larger, overarching factors that have contributed to the decline of unions.

1. The hollowing-out of the country's manufacturing base and, with it, a decline in those industry jobs which, historically, had not only been strongly organized but well paid. We're speaking mainly of the automobile, steel, paper, and heavy equipment industries.

Even the auto industry, represented by the estimable United Auto Workers (UAW)—one of the most successful and innovative unions in American history—took tremendous hits during the seventies and eighties, losing hundreds of thousands of members.

Americans are still buying cars and trucks at a brisk pace, but it no longer even registers as "news" that foreign markets have decimated U.S. sales. That is now a "given." And those Japanese auto companies that have set up shop in the U.S. made certain to situate their plants in right-to-work states in the Deep South, areas hostile to organized labor.

If we subtract all the non-manufacturing and service jobs (nurses, civil servants, police and firemen, teachers, etc.), there are barely 6% of union workers engaged in the manufacture of products. When you lose your base you can't expect to maintain your membership. Worse news: Unless something momentous and unforeseen occurs, it's unlikely we're ever going to get these industries back to anything approaching their previous numbers. That era, along with the quality jobs and UAW glory that went with it, is over.

2. Government has assumed custody of key union provisions. From overtime pay to hours of work, to guaranteed days off and employees' rights and standards, laws have been passed by the state and federal governments to address such issues. Government has effectively co-opted much of what only union contracts traditionally did.

For example, where joining a union was once the only way to get premium pay for overtime, or "penalty pay" for showing up and being sent home when there was no work, those goodies are now mandated by state and federal statutes.

Safety is another example. Where it once required specific language in a union contract to insure that a workplace was safe and secure, the passage, in 1970, of the Occupation Health and Safety Act (OSHA), made every employer in the country accountable to a federal safety code. Today, an employee need only pick up the phone and dial OSHA's number to complain about an unsafe working condition and, chances are, he will be placed in contact with a field agent.

Tangentially, many businesses manage to keep unions out by providing their employees with comparable wages and benefits. Even though union wages are still significantly higher, across the board, than non-union wages, many companies are able to keep out unions by providing compensation and benefits (vacations, pensions, health insurance) that compare favorably to those of union shops, thus obviating the need for organizing.

What hurts most in these cases is that the people ("free riders") receiving these comparable wages and benefits think they're making it on their own, without having to rely on a union. In truth, without the existence of unions, there's no telling how low base wages for unskilled blue-collar work would fall, with nothing to prop them up except the federal minimum wage.

3. Changes in demographics and culture. There is a decreased respect for the role of organized labor, for its founders, its battles, its overall narrative, and an alarming lack of interest in labor's political and social implications.

High school history and civic textbooks of the Baby Boomer generation (and the one preceding it) routinely included accounts of the achievements of labor leaders such as Samuel Gompers, John L. Lewis, Walter Reuther, et al, mentioning them in much the same way they mentioned political leaders and social reformers.

Today, it would be ludicrous to expect a high school history text to single out specific contemporary labor leaders who've made a difference—unless it was something scandalous or bizarre (e.g., the disappearance of Jimmy Hoffa).

Arguably, we've also witnessed a marked decline in our sense of community. This can be seen in the fact that fewer people are willing to march in Labor Day parades, or enroll in social clubs or civic organizations, or attend community events.

And there is a obvious spillover into politics. Today, everybody seems to want to call himself an independent rather than a Republican or Democrat, having grown increasingly frustrated with the traditional two-party system. The same sense of faux-independence applies to working people as well. Workers prefer to think of themselves as incipient, yet-to-be-realized entrepreneurs rather than proletarian toilers.

Identifying oneself as part of a larger entity—a union, a community, even a neighborhood—no longer holds the appeal it once did, just as collectivism no longer makes as much sense as it once did. With everyone's sights set on upward mobility, fewer people are comfortable publicly identifying themselves as blue-collar, because doing so cuts them off from the prestige that comes from lucrative jobs/careers.

With those values now in play, who the hell wants to march down Main Street in a Labor Day parade wearing union colors?

There's an anecdote told about John D. Rockefeller which reflects this change in cultural attitudes. It occurred during the Depression. A group of poor people congregated outside the gate of Rockefeller's mansion, and began banging the covers of his metal trash cans and shouting insults, making a terrible racket.

The police were summoned. But because the police were sympathetic to the demonstrators, they waited several minutes, watching the protest with interest, before breaking up the demonstration. Their deep-seated sympathies lay with the protesters.

Today, that it episode would play out differently. Besides poor people not having to access to a wealthy industrialist's home (he'd be isolated inside a gated estate, with his own private security force patrolling the place), it's unlikely the city police would react sympathetically.

Rather, they'd treat the demonstrators like criminal trespassers and drive them away, possibly arrest them. They would likely treat them with contempt. Why? Because working people don't have the core respect they once had. Simple as that.

CounterPunch
2008

PATRIOTISM AND THE LABOR MOVEMENT

There's an undeniable truth which, if properly publicized, could make unions look pretty damn good even to those rabid Sarah Palin-Joe the Plumber fans out there. Simply put: Union workers tend to be wildly patriotic Americans. Sometimes, they even go overboard in their patriotic love of country. Sometimes they go so far as to demand that their loyalty be reciprocated.

Given labor's unabashed patriotism, especially in light of all the flag-waving, "country first" propaganda being circulated by the anti-union Republican party, it's surprising that organized labor hasn't responded with a splashy "pro-American" campaign of its own. As corny and "beneath their dignity" as that idea might initially appear, the AFL-CIO and Change to Win should seriously consider it.

They should offer this little quiz. They should ask our citizens who's the more "patriotic" American:

* The investment banker who shelters money in off-shore accounts to avoid paying his fair share of U.S. taxes, and cares nothing about how the country as a whole is doing, so long as he's rolling in dough?

* The business owner who ships his operation overseas in order to reap higher profits from lower labor costs, helping to put money in a foreign government's coffers while, simultaneously, depriving hard-working Americans of their jobs?

* The defense contractor who talks the talk, waves the American flag, and professes to put "country first," but who cheats the American taxpayer by criminally overcharging for his services and products, all in the name of "Keeping America Strong"?

* The politician who has allowed America's infrastructure (its highways, waterways, and bridges) to deteriorate to alarming levels, all because he'd rather invest public money in Wall Street

than in the mundane and less profitable enterprise of maintaining the upkeep of the United States?

* Or the union member—the dues-paying man or woman—who works in this country, spends all of his money in this country, pays his fair share of taxes to this country, marches in parades celebrating the glory of this country, and wants nothing more than to keep this country as strong and proud as he or she remembers or imagines it?

Who's the more patriotic American?

If one aspect of patriotism involves a willingness to perform national service, consider: More union members have served in the military than have bankers, accountants, lawyers, professors, artists or professional politicians. That's a fact.

Perhaps the argument can be made that military service doesn't really matter. If that's the case, if military service shouldn't be seen as a noble endeavor, then fine, let's have the politicians shut up about it. But if it is considered a worthy national sacrifice, then let's be clear about who it is who's doing the actual sacrificing.

More than your entrepreneurs, corporate executives, or hedge fund managers, union workers intuitively recognize the importance of pulling together to make the country stronger. Unlike the professional or "moneyed" crowd, union people don't engage in eloquent rhetoric or pay lip service to it, even as they look for ways to avoid it. No, union folks actually do it.

And their patriotism isn't the abstract or ornamental variety, the kind that exists mainly "in principle." It's the genuine article. Scoff all you like at their naivete or gullibility or gushy sentimentality, but you cut open a union member's arm, and it bleeds red, white and blue.

Organized labor needs to publicize this fact. It needs to turn this whole "love of country" issue—which hypocritical Republicans are using to bludgeon the Democrats—into something that can benefit the unions.

Not only would portraying union workers as being America's fiercest and most loyal patriots be an effective campaign device, it would have the additional virtue of being absolutely true.

CounterPunch
2008

OBAMA AND THE RULING CLASS

> "We don't pay taxes. Only the little people pay taxes."
> —Leona Helmsley

The list of Obama nominees not to have paid their taxes continues to grow. The latest confessor is Kathleen Sebelius, governor of Kansas, former state representative, former insurance honcho, and Obama's nominee for Secretary of Health and Human Services (HHS). On March 31, it was revealed that Sebelius had "forgotten" to pay almost $8,000 in taxes. Oops.

Earlier, Tom Daschle—former South Dakota senator, former Senate Majority Leader, Obama's original choice for HHS Secretary, and a man generally regarded as the one person in the country capable of ushering in a national health care plan— turned out to owe so much in unpaid taxes he was forced to withdraw.

Daschle, a corporate lobbyist (despite how hard they tried to "spin" his position, when you make $2 million in one year from industry fees, that's what you are, a *lobbyist*) owed more than $128,000 in unpaid taxes. His withdrawal was a stunning disappointment to the administration.

During confirmation proceedings, Timothy Geithner, our Secretary of the Treasury, was forced to go on national television and apologize for not having paid over $34,000 in taxes. The man who, as Treasury Secretary, would be the titular head of the Internal Revenue Service apparently didn't know how to fill out his tax form.

Nancy Killefer, Obama's nominee for Chief Performance Officer, also had to withdraw due to tax problems. She threw in the towel with the investigation barely underway, choosing to nip it in the bud before too much was revealed. No thanks, she said. You can keep your appointment and I'll keep my privacy. *Adios.*

And Ron Kirk, Obama's choice for U.S. Trade Rep, was shown to owe $10,000 in back taxes, which he agreed to pay only after it was made clear that his appointment to a big-time government position was contingent upon repayment. Makes you wonder how amenable he and the others would have been to making restitution had their appointments not hung in the balance.

These were the ones we actually *heard* about, the ones who had made it all the way to final cut, the ones whose names had been formally submitted as nominees. It doesn't take into account those who, presumably, were removed from consideration when red flags went up in the first round of vetting, or those who dropped out voluntarily after meeting with their tax accountants.

Of course, it's possible, as some have suggested, that these wealthy people were the victims of red tape, that the complexity of the U.S. tax code is the real culprit here. Yes, that's possible. Still, it's odd how these people always err on the side of paying too little than too much. How refreshing it would be for an audit to reveal that someone making millions of dollars had actually paid a few thousand too much.

Unfortunately, the opportunity for President Obama to step up to the plate was lost here. Instead of immediately withdrawing the name of any nominee who'd shown they failed to pay their taxes, and making it clear that he wanted honest, fair-minded people in his administration, he took the other approach. He became complicit in providing cover and excuses.

The opportunity to prove that he fully intended to "change" the way Washington did business, beginning with flushing out the smug, the slippery, the uber-privileged, was ignored. It could have been a defining moment not only for Obama, but for the country. Instead, he demonstrated that his allegiance lay with the powers that be.

This whole thing should have been embarrassing for everyone— not only the people caught "cheating" on their taxes, but for Obama's advisors as well. But, wild ambition being what it is, these revelations were more or less shrugged off. Those who talked their way out of it have prestigious government jobs, and

those who were dropped from consideration have already
moved on with their careers.

Still, critics of the administration will surely say that the reason
rich liberals don't mind Obama's plan to raise taxes on the
wealthy is because they have no intention of paying them. And
we sink deeper into cynicism.

CounterPunch
2009

SENATOR SHELBY NEEDS DETROIT TO FAIL

Most of us are able to tolerate the politics of someone we disagree with, so long as his arguments are sincere and civil, and his beliefs are demonstrably consistent, rational and principled in nature.

A "pro-life" advocate who happens to be a pacifist (a Quaker, say), an anti-war demonstrator and an anti-capital punishment zealot, is someone we could learn to abide. We may not agree with his views on abortion but, given their context, we can understand them and, on some level, respect them.

But the person who wants to recriminalize abortion—yet favors the death penalty, supports American wars of aggression, ignored Pope John Paul II's objection to the U.S. invasion of Iraq (while clinging to the Church's position on abortion), and walks the earth as a veritable Exterminator—is a whole other deal.

It's no coincidence that in Dante's "Inferno," the hypocrites, frauds, liars and "evil counselors" were consigned to a lower depth of Hell than those who committed violence to others and themselves—the murderers and suicides.

Which brings us to Senator Richard Shelby of Alabama, ranking Republican on the Senate Banking, Housing and Urban Affairs Committee. Lately, Senator Shelby has been talking out of both sides of his mouth—on the one hand, pretending to care about Detroit's welfare, and, on the other hand, nurturing an ambitious, opposing agenda.

At hearings in November, 2008, Shelby piously expressed his sympathy for the terrible jam Detroit's Big Three automakers got themselves into (i.e., massive debt, plummeting sales), but said that, despite their troubles, he couldn't, in good conscience, agree to spend taxpayer money on an enterprise that seemed destined to fail—not without some radical changes.

Among the changes Shelby suggested was asking the UAW (United Auto Workers) to more or less capitulate—to give back everything they'd gained over the last 30 years. Of course, this was something that not only *wasn't* going to happen (the union had already made dozens of unilateral concessions), but something Shelby himself *didn't want* to happen.

In truth, Shelby's objections were based not on fiduciary responsibility, but venal self-interest. Shelby wants Detroit to fail. He needs it to fail. His phony display of sympathy and so-called "restructuring plan" were as bogus as the ultimatum George W. Bush gave Saddam Hussein before we invaded Iraq, telling him to leave the country within 48 hours or face the consequences.

As if Saddam would actually abdicate the presidency, pack up his family and possessions, hang a "Gone Fishin'" sign on the palace door, and book it out of there for parts unknown—all because Bush asked him to. It was a transparent provocation. Bush knew he wouldn't do it, which is precisely why he asked. Shelby is doing the same thing with Detroit. If the man had an ounce of integrity, he would come clean and state his real motives.

Shelby's reasons for wanting Detroit to fail are breathtakingly parochial. Not only has he received significant campaign donations from foreign automakers, Alabama is home to several foreign auto companies (including a billion-dollar Hyundai plant outside Montgomery) who were lured there by its relatively low standard of living, friendly pollution standards, and prickly anti-union sensibilities.

Moreover, Alabama has given these manufacturers *billions* of dollars in subsidies, tax breaks, bonuses, and other perks as inducements to relocate. These companies not only don't pay taxes, the state has built new roads and highways and expanded the railroad to accommodate their plants, and offered to do their employee hiring and training for free. Alabama is aggressively on the hustle. It's all about jobs.

The same goes for Tennessee, Mississippi, Georgia, Kentucky, South Carolina and Texas. Indeed, the South envisions itself launching the greatest "post-industrial" industrial explosion in

American history, an Auto Renaissance of sorts, with hundreds of thousands of good jobs transforming the South into the manufacturing juggernaut the Midwest and Northeast used to be.

Remember those jokes about how Japan may have technically won World War II, after all—via Toyota, Nissan and Honda dominating the American auto market? Well, the South may have won the Civil War, 140 years after the fact, by leaving those Yankee Rust Belt manufacturing economies in the dust. How ironic would that be?

Of course, for that to happen, Detroit and the UAW need to be destroyed. And so far, everything is right on schedule.

The Exception Magazine
2009

WORKPLACE VIOLENCE

We've all read those tragic, terrifying accounts of employees who walk into their office or factory, pull out a gun and begin shooting people. While they're frequently portrayed as disgruntled, mentally unstable employees who've been recently reprimanded or terminated, more often than not (because so many end up killing themselves), their motive remains a mystery.

Confoundingly, these crimes involve seemingly "regular" people who appear to have simply "snapped." As a former labor union rep, I've personally witnessed dozens of people suspended or fired from their jobs for a variety of reasons (mostly for chronic absenteeism, the number one cause of terminations in the U.S.), and have never seen anyone commit a violent act directed toward another person; not at the meeting itself, not at any time afterward.

The closest anyone ever came to scaring people In the room during a discharge meeting was when a maintenance man, who was being fired for insurance fraud, kicked over a chair on his way out. I'd be lying if I said the incident wasn't a bit unnerving. The chair was a sturdy, good-sized one, and he kicked the living hell out of it, sent it skittering across the room.

In truth, emotional displays—much less physical violence—at termination meetings are rare. As traumatic and shattering as economic homicide is, for whatever reason, people (both men and women) don't even cry when they get the news. In fact, they usually remain preternaturally calm, almost stoical.

What happens when people are told they're fired is that they listen grimly to the words being spoken while staring at a fixed spot on the floor or on the wall a few inches above the speaker's head. They fixate on that spot. Typically, there are no outbursts or histrionics. If I had to identify the most common response, I'd say it was one of profound embarrassment and shame.

When the meeting is over and these people realize they are no longer employed, they walk out of the room in an awkward, trance-like state. Many of them try to hold a tight smile. They're escorted to their locker by a security guard, scrutinized as they remove their personal stuff, and then led out to their car. Even when it's people who deserve to be fired, it's a brutal, merciless, and heart-wrenching thing to witness.

There's an odd corollary to this. People do, in fact, *cry* at some of these meetings. But they tend to do it when they enter the HR office fully expecting to be fired, then find out they aren't. They cry when they're told they're being given a reprieve. That's when the tears flow. When they learn they've kept their job.

Morbid as this may sound, whenever there was a news story of some guy murdering fellow workers, people at the union hall would speculate as to who among the facility's several hundred employees would be most apt to do something like that—come in blasting. This guessing-game was done partly as an exercise in dark humor, partly as a means of trying to make sense of something senseless.

Our union executive board still remembered the UAW (United Auto Workers) shooting some years earlier, where a fired employee pulled a gun from his lunch box and killed a Human Resource manager and a production supervisor, leaving two terrified union reps unharmed. Not to make light of what was clearly a horrific tragedy, but our take on the incident was purely practical: at least the shooter, unstable as he was, could differentiate between the good guys and the bad guys.

Obviously, no one ever anticipates anything like this ever happening. Indeed, the one thing you *never* hear in response to a workplace shooting is people asserting that they had predicted the person would do it ("Yep, we all knew it was only a matter of time before Fred came in here and shot some folks."). It doesn't happen that way.

Perverse as these impromptu "profiling" sessions may have been, they regularly yielded the same two unedifying theories:

First, it was always a male who was the potential shooter, because women don't do this sort of thing. Second, it was always a quiet, reserved man, and never a talkative, gregarious fellow.

Ultimately, what we concluded was that it was hopeless trying to guess who was most likely to come in with a gun. Despite all our speculation, only one category of employee was ever eliminated—that of the demonstrably sociable "people person." Which narrowed the list of suspects to about 90% of the male population of the facility.

Identifying "probable violence" is close to impossible. Sure, it's easy to connect the dots when you're working backwards, after the bloody deed has been done, but it's a whole other deal trying to predict one.

Unless the guy is uttering threats or ominous warnings, no one can know what's going on inside someone's head. Men with volcanic tempers will punch holes in the wall, and mild-mannered men will come in with guns. And vice versa.

Arguably, the only "guaranteed" way of preventing a workplace shooting is to become intolerably invasive. You intensify security by installing metal detectors, having armed guards stationed in the facility and conducting random searches. To stop the 0.00001 percent of the population who actually does this stuff, you treat the other 99.99999 percent as potential murderers.

I recently received a letter from an outfit called the "Homeland Defense Journal," inviting me to attend a 2-day seminar (on January 28 and 29, 2009) in Arlington, Virginia, entitled, "Managing Workplace Violence Workshop."

According to the brochure, these were among the topics to be covered:

- "How to create or improve your workplace violence prevention policy and program (you will actually create a policy as part of the course)

- How to recognize the early warning signs of potential violence and how to appropriately intervene to address them.
- How to improve employee reporting of threats and incidents.
- How to access your organization to detect problems that can contribute to creating a violence prone work environment
- How to deal with a hostile employee and clam the person down using the Stay Calm method
- What to do if confronted with the threat of violence
- How to create an effective workplace violence crisis response plan."

The registration fees for the 2-day affair were:
Government: $599
Small Business: $699
Industry: $799.
(Isn't it interesting that "Government," typically regarded as a source of plentiful, readily available money, is offered the cheapest rate?)

Nothing against the good folks at Homeland Defense Journal, but I can't interpret their agenda as anything other than well-meaning propaganda. Frightening and traumatic as workplace violence is, there doesn't seem to be a reliable, non-draconian way of preventing it.

Of course, we all realize that, for our protection, businesses must continue to seek creative approaches, and for that effort they should be commended. Still, despite all the ambitious psychological profiling and seminar-babble, one can't help but view these attempts as wishful thinking.

CounterPunch
2008

IN PURSUIT OF THE LABOR VOTE

"I could hire one-half of the working class to kill the other half."
—Jay Gould, Wall Street financier, 1886

It's not a happy time for labor unions. The institution that gave us the weekend, vacations, pensions and health insurance, and is credited with having more or less "invented" the middle-class, is now viewed, at best, as anachronistic and lame, and, at worst, as parasitic and corrupt.

If Wes Craven were to make a horror movie about the economy, unions would be cast as the zombies. We walk the earth, we are sentient, we appear menacing; but we are neither alive nor dead. We are the American economy's Undead.

Unless there's a strike or racketeering scandal (or another rumor that they found Jimmy Hoffa's body), organized labor tends to be ignored by politicians and mainstream media. There's nothing particularly revealing in this neglect, other than showing that garden-variety union business doesn't generate much interest—not among the movers and shakers, not among the moved and the shaken.

This all changes come election time. Every four years, like clockwork, unions get nudged into the limelight, as national audiences are treated to media analyses and predictions of that coveted, elusive prize: the "labor vote." And 2008 will be no exception.

During the 2004 primaries, as Democratic candidates toured the factories and union halls of Blue states—with the AFL-CIO remaining tantalizingly uncommitted, its 13 million members awaiting their "marching orders"—there was intense speculation over who would win labor's endorsement. ABC's Peter Jennings called Howard Dean "labor's man." CNN's Chris Matthews said Richard Gephardt was labor's "best friend." PBS's Mark Shields described John Kerry's labor record as "tepid."

Although the AFL-CIO—organized labor's version of the Pentagon—cautiously withheld its endorsement until fairly late in the campaign (when it declared, anti-climatically, for Kerry), several prominent unions had come out early and aggressively for Gephardt and Dean, well in advance of the targeted Iowa caucus.

Iowa had been advertised as a showdown between the stolidly protectionist, anti-NAFTA Gephardt (who had won in Iowa in 1988), supported by steelworkers, machinists and other "smoke-stack" industries, and the ultra-hip Dean, whose endorsement by the American Federation of State, County and Municipal Employees (AFSCME) and the Service Employees International Union (SEIU), America's largest union, was supposed to signal a sea change in labor's national agenda.

Of course, instead of a union-driven victory for either Dean or Gephardt, Mr. Blue State himself, John Kerry, pulled off the upset, contributing to front-runner Dean's stunning fall from grace, and Gephardt's abrupt departure (he withdrew two days later).

What the Iowa Democrats did was no surprise. They did what defiant working people have been doing for 40 years—exposing bloc-voting for labor candidates as the urban myth it is. Indeed, anyone who still believes that "friends of labor" are less apt than the average voter to flex their political independence hasn't been paying attention.

Those "Reagan-Bush '84" bumper stickers seen in union parking lots—even in the wake of Reagan's peremptory firing of 11,000 striking air-traffic controllers—didn't get there by accident. They were put there to show union muckety-mucks that the membership doesn't give a flying gee whiz about "trickle down" solidarity. No one's going to tell them how to vote, thank you very much. Which is a pity.

For the record, there hasn't been anything resembling a unified labor vote since 1964, when LBJ crushed Barry Goldwater. This was back in labor's glory days, when membership hovered at 30% (it's 12% today), when the UAW faced negligible foreign competition, and the International Brotherhood of Teamsters still ruled America's highways.

But by 1972, following years of radical politics and social upheaval, it had become apparent that the Democratic Party, long regarded as labor's patron saint and benefactor, had drifted so far to the cultural left, become so diffuse and confoundedly "inclusive," that it no longer automatically spoke for the rank-and-file.

As a consequence, unions found themselves representing a new breed of member: the fiercely independent, anti-corporate, pro-labor, anti-Communist, "Roosevelt Republican." A walking-talking ideological paradox.

Accordingly, as union members openly bailed on the Party, the Democrats returned the favor, withdrawing their support of labor's core agenda, and running for cover the moment anyone accused them of being "anti-business" (the Mark of Cain in politics). Even academe, long an ideological ally of the labor movement, eventually lost interest.

That awkward juxtaposition of Chardonnay-intellectuals and the beer-and-pretzel crowd had always been suspect, bringing to mind Oscar Wilde's description of an English fox hunt: "The unspeakable in pursuit of the inedible." In any case, today's left-wing academics seem to have more sympathy for Turkish dissident poets than striking auto workers.

So, how much influence will an AFL-CIO's endorsement have in '08? Arguably, it will fall somewhere between the Teamsters' historic embracing of Ronald Reagan, in 1980, and the UAW's perfunctory nod to Michael Dukakis, in 1988. In other words, it's anyone's guess, as always. Which is a pity.

Philadelphia Inquirer
2004

THE FREE RIDER PROBLEM

Union membership in the United States hovers at approximately 12%, down from an all-time high of about 35%, a figure reached during organized labor's glory days, back in the early 1950s. Startlingly, in just five decades labor has lost two-thirds of its membership. Even more sobering, if we look only at the private sector, and don't count government employees, school teachers, firemen and policemen, union membership dips under 7%. Understandably, these numbers terrify organized labor.

But it can be argued that these figures are somewhat misleading. There's a dynamic in play which supports the argument that organized labor's influence is significantly greater than the naked statistics indicate. That dynamic is the phenomenon of the "free rider." Simply put, free riders are those workers who benefit from the existence of labor unions, who reap many of the goodies provided by union contracts, but who don't belong to a union.

Free riders come in two forms: those who work for a company which, in order to keep the union out, offers wages and benefits that come close to union standards; and those workers who belong to an "agency shop," an arrangement where workers are represented by a labor union but whose employees are not *required* to join, and who, therefore, even though they benefit from the wages and benefits negotiated by the union, do not show up on its membership rolls. School districts are a common source of agency shops.

While the number of agency shop "non-members" are dutifully recorded, it's impossible to quantify the number of free riders who fall into the other category—those who work at non-union facilities which offer wages and benefits close to union levels. But the number is considerable. Paying a decent wage and offering decent benefits is an enormous inducement to keep people from seeking union affiliation; and it's a step that companies which are adamantly opposed to unions are willing to take.

Arguably, from a noble point of view, if it's the role of unions to improve the economic lives of working people, then unions are succeeding, if indirectly, by motivating non-union companies to reward their employees. After all, securing workers decent wages and benefits is what it's all about. The downside, of course, is that these workers don't pay union dues, don't appear on membership rolls, and, worst of all, live their lives under the delusion that they've made it "on their own."

Free riders don't realize that if it weren't for the existence of labor unions, forklift drivers wouldn't be earning $20 per hour. If it weren't for labor unions, working people would be scraping by, undercutting each other in the open job market, with management in the position of calling the shots, able to appeal to the lowest common denominator.

Why are companies willing to pay higher wages and offer benefits to keep the union out? Because they don't want the kind of "partnership" that comes with a union shop. They don't want to have to negotiate a contract every three or four years; they don't want the grievance/arbitration procedure introduced; they don't a workforce of people who see the union (rather than the company) as its benefactor.

But free riders (most of them, at least) don't see it that way; they believe that making a living wage and enjoying decent benefits is something they've somehow "earned." At the risk of making a grotesque generalization, the American South stands as a prime example. The reason corporations set up factories and offices in the South is because they know that Southern workers are staunchly anti-collectivist, less apt than workers anywhere in the country to seek to join or form a labor union.

Yes, the standard of living in the South is lower, and yes, environmental restrictions are less strict; but businesses know that by offering wages and benefits within spitting distance of union standards, making the decision to join up even less attractive, they can keep their employees non-union. This knowledge has even reached Tokyo. That's why Japan has established their auto plants and other ventures in the deep South.

But without the presence of unions, these free riders would be facing an alternative, far harsher reality. Without the "threat" of unions, they would be devoid of leverage, forced to navigate the job market on their own. Admittedly, some of these free riders have come to recognize the dynamic, and have used the threat of joining a union as a means of gaining monetarily. More power to them. They may not be paying dues or appearing on national membership rolls, but they are advancing themselves economically, and doing it, indirectly, with the help of organized labor.

So that 12% figure is a bit misleading. What that number would be if we factored in all those workers who, while not members themselves, benefited from the existence of labor unions is anyone's guess. But all we have to do is look around to see that it would be significant.

CounterPunch
2007

WAL-MART REDUX

Calling Wal-Mart Stores, Inc. a leading retailer is like calling the Pacific Ocean a large body of water. Over the course of 30 years, Wal-Mart has become an icon, a phenomenon, a household word around the world. It has 60 stores in Communist China. It's the largest private employer in Mexico and Canada, as well as the U.S. Tangentially, it's also become a symbolic thorn in the side of organized labor. Actually, it's more than a thorn; it's a metaphorical dagger in labor's heart.

Back when Wal-Mart had a "mere" 3,600 stores in the U.S. (there are 4,000 today), the AFL-CIO launched an aggressive organizing drive, looking to crack the company's impenetrable anti-union shell. Yet, despite bringing all of its formidable resources to bear, the House of Labor could not convince the employees of a single Wal-Mart store—not one!—to join the union. As a consequence, Wal-Mart further solidified its mystique as being more or less "union proof."

In truth, the record hasn't been quite that dismal. Over the years there have been a handful of Wal-Mart stores in Canada that voted to join a union. Alas, the only one to do so in the U.S. was quickly shut down by the company (an indication of how vehemently anti-union their management is).

But let's give Wal-Mart employees some credit. They aren't stupid. It's not that they can't see the advantages of joining a labor union. What prevents these workers from signing union cards isn't ignorance, but *fear*—the fear of losing their jobs, the fear that the company will close up shop and move to another location if they go union, or will fire people who are caught circulating union literature.

At Wal-Mart it's understood that if the bosses catch you passing out union pamphlets, they fire you, and if they catch you reading union material, they threaten you. But isn't it illegal to discharge an employee for disseminating union literature? Of course it is. It's a clear violation of federal labor law, and Wal-Mart knows it.

The problem is, not only are unfair labor practice charges (ULPs) hard to prove in court, but a company with Wal-Mart's muscle isn't going to worry about something as petty as an obscure labor statute. Even if they get nailed a few times (which they have), they're willing to risk it. Wal-Mart has found that the public relations backlash to getting hit with the occasional ULP is miniscule.

However, the future isn't necessarily as grim as it seems. Indeed, there's a scenario by which Wal-Mart's employees not only organize themselves, but coalesce to form a union of their own. With their staggering number of employees nationwide, a union composed exclusively of Wal-Mart workers could easily become one of the largest in America. In this scenario the employees rise up and lead a renaissance—a Great Renewal—of union activism and influence.

And no, it's not a fairy tale.

First, a quick look at what happened to the labor movement. Arguably, there were two crushing blows that put it on the ropes: one was an increase in aggressive, anti-union tactics by American corporations, traceable to President Reagan's sudden firing of 11,000 air traffic controllers, in 1981; and the other was the loss of, literally, millions of well-paid, richly-benefited jobs in the manufacturing sector, the majority of which were unionized.

These jobs—in the auto industry, in steel, rubber, timber, furniture, heavy equipment, pulp and saw mills, etc.—were ones that generated considerable purchasing power. They were jobs that afforded employees new homes and new cars, jobs into which sons and daughters proudly followed their fathers. It's no exaggeration to say that these same jobs were responsible for "inventing" the middle-class.

Today, however, the mantra you keep hearing is that the United States has shifted from a manufacturing economy to a "service economy." Accordingly, the unions that have continued to prosper are the "service" unions, those whose workers are immune to having their jobs co-opted or sent overseas:

teachers, nurses, pilots, longshoremen, police and firemen, truckers, carpenters and the like.

Although we still build cars in this country, the combination of foreign brands cutting into the U.S. market and manufacturing plants moving to the anti-union Southern states have decimated the UAW (United Auto Workers). Overall union membership in the U.S. has dropped from a high of 35% (during the 1950s) to about 12% today. And no group has experienced a more dramatic wipe-out than the UAW.

But there's another, generally overlooked classification of "service" worker that is also immune to being absorbed or having its work shipped off to a foreign country. It's the retail clerks. They're the ones who man the checkout stands, deal with the customers, stock the shelves, and generally keep the store running. They're the people who work at Wal-Mart.

Yes, retail clerks sort of have (or had) a union already. But the original Retail Clerks Union was never taken seriously; it merged with the Amalgamated Meat Cutters almost 30 years ago and became the United Food and Commercial Workers (UFCW).

Today, the non-grocery retail clerks are pretty much left hanging out there on their own, ripe for mobilization. If America's "big boy" unions (autos, steel, heavy equipment) were brought to their knees by the effects of globalization, it's not unreasonable to suggest that labor's less glamorous but well-insulated "little brothers" resume the fight.

Consider: What would happen if Wal-Mart employees were to throw down the gauntlet? What would happen if, all across the country, they simultaneously announced that they were going to seek union affiliation—either by joining an existing union or forming one of their own—and *dared* the company to try and stop them?

Wouldn't such a splashy public declaration (via full-page ads in major newspapers, TV and radio) prevent Wal-Mart from using any sneaky tricks to thwart the union drive? Wouldn't the national attention prevent management from resorting to its usual tactics of illegal threats and intimidation?

In addition to paying for the newspaper and other media spots, the AFL-CIO (or, more likely, Change To Win) could be counted upon to provide free legal representation to anyone who was fired for his or her union involvement. Organized labor's legal defense team lives for moments like this. Moreover, with so many of its 4,000 stores involved, Wal-Mart wouldn't have the option of shutting down those units that voted to go union. There simply would be too many of them.

The fact that retail clerks can't be swallowed up or outsourced needs to be seen as more than just a lucky break. It's a circumstance which, if played right, can be converted into genuine leverage. Wal-Mart's magnitude, high profile, and dependency upon a mega-sized workforce are the very components which, ironically, make it vulnerable to a spontaneous uprising.

Think about it. If Wal-Mart's workers publicly announced—in front of God, Pete Seeger, and the Department of Labor—their intention to unionize, what could Wal-Mart management (legally) do to prevent them? With so much sunshine let in, any move they made would be subject to intense scrutiny. The employees' declaration would have the moral authority of Ronald Reagan's famous, "Mr. Gorbachev, tear down this wall!"

And it's not just Wal-Marters who have this opportunity laid before them. With the luxury of knowing that their jobs can't be pulled out from under them, the retail clerks at Target, Starbucks, Home Depot, et al, would also have the power to drop the hammer.

Audacious as it sounds, America's retail clerks, if mobilized, could be the ones to reinvigorate the labor movement. Crazier things have happened.

CounterPunch
2008

CAFTA'S BLOODTRAILS

On Wednesday, April 23, a complaint was filed with the U.S. Department of Labor by U.S. and Guatemalan labor groups, claiming that the workers' rights provisions of CAFTA (Central American Free Trade Agreement) were being violated. The petitioners allege that union members in Guatemala were not only being routinely harassed, threatened and intimidated, but that assassinations of union leaders have occurred.

Since 2006, when Guatemala became a trading partner in CAFTA (whose other signatories include the U.S., Dominican Republic, Honduras, El Salvador, Costa Rica and Nicaragua), eight trade unionists have been killed. The most sensational murder occurred in January, 2007, when Pedro Zamora, the charismatic president of a port union, was brazenly gunned down in front of his home by a carload of assailants in broad daylight.

Five separate complaints were filed on Wednesday, alleging violations against members of six unions affiliated with agriculture, seaport shipping and textile industries. The complaints seek punitive damages from the Guatemalan government—a remedy "guaranteed" by CAFTA's workers' protection language. These fines can run as high as $15 million per year. As to the prospect of the Guatemalan government actually being found guilty and having to fork over the money, no one is holding their breath.

A stunning fact: While there have been dozens of formal complaints filed by labor organizations and human rights groups since 1994 (when the first of these agreements was implemented), not a single one has resulted In sanctions against the alleged offenders. After conducting what they described as "thorough investigations," the U.S. Department of Labor announced that it had found no violations. None. In other words, so far, every trading partner in the world has a perfect, *unblemished* human rights record. What were the odds?

It's time we asked ourselves, Which of those so-called "free trade" agreements have actually fulfilled their ambitious promises to recognize workers' rights and protect the environment? Which countries, if any, have made an effort to live up to the ambitious, idealistic language contained in those provisions? By "live up to," we mean provide evidence that the government is willing to vigorously prosecute businesses who are in violation.

It's also time that we acknowledged a simple, discouraging fact: In countries where labor unions are violently opposed by government and business interests, a treaty isn't likely to make much difference. Businesses and their government cronies will find a way to get around the wording. Consider: Have Mexican labor unions flourished under NAFTA? Have Honduran labor unions flourished under CAFTA (Central American Free Trade Agreement)? Have Latin American workers at the bottom of the economic ladder benefited significantly from "free trade"?

In truth, whether NAFTA, CAFTA or the proposed U.S.-Colombia Free Trade Agreement, it was a consortium of financial and manufacturing interests who initially pushed for these deals, and who did so for reasons that were not only largely incompatible with workers' rights and environmental protection, but, in many cases, in direct contradiction to them.

While we're at it, we need to acknowledge another fact: These trade agreements were glorified money grabs, plain and simple. They were *business deals.* As for the "human rights" and environmental provisions spelled out in their language, those were merely palliatives, a means of getting them approved by Congress. Does anyone really believe that maintaining the viability of labor unions even entered into the equation?

Of course, what you hear from free trade proponents is that, imperfect as they may be, these trade agreements are the only means we have of fixing a bad situation. Without them, the U.S. would have no legal right to intervene in a country's commerce. Indeed, without the existence of CAFTA, that formal complaint filed last Wednesday would not have been possible.

According to free trade advocates, these trade agreements offer the U.S. the "human rights" leverage it never before had.

While this argument may be true in principle, in the real world it's not only false and misleading, it's insulting. If the respective governments (including the U.S.) are unwilling to *enforce* the provisions of the law—despite the "opportunity" for interested parties to file their petitions—those provisions are all but meaningless.

Worse, being on the books in the form it is, this language implies that the situation has improved and that the necessary steps are being taken, which is untrue. This argument is also amusing, in that it exposes the ways in which American politicians and businessmen cherry-pick their positions.

Take the anti-Communist hard-liners, for instance. They objected to the U.S. signing arms limitation treaties with the Soviet Union on the grounds that the Russkies couldn't be trusted to uphold their end of the bargain. But these are the same people who are falling over themselves trying to get these free-trade agreements ratified, even when there is *zero* evidence that the signatory governments have any intention of adhering to the human rights requirements.

Similarly, many of these free trade fundamentalists ("We need to *engage* these regimes, not snub them!") are the same people, the very same zealous holdouts, who, for decades, have opposed lifting the trade embargo with Cuba. Apparently, those snappy, "let's engage these regimes" arguments didn't apply when it came to Fidel Castro. Go figure.

We need to drop the pretense and get real. Why should we expect a coalition of big business and government to consider giving labor unions a fair shake, particularly in Latin American countries, where (as it once was in the U.S.) government-sanctioned violence against unions is standard procedure?

We have to stop feigning shock and disappointment when these treaty provisions are violated. That certain countries continue to terrorize labor unions should not come as a surprise. The only "surprise" is that an outside observer would honestly believe these governments ever had the slightest intention of complying . . . or that the U.S. would risk throwing a wrench in the works by punishing a valued trading partner.

CounterPunch
2008

WHEN WORKERS' RIGHTS GO UNENFORCED

"The Law, in its majestic equality, forbids the rich, as well
as the poor, to sleep under the bridges, to beg in the
streets, and to steal."
                                        —Anatole France

Given the dramatic changes in the political landscape, there's a
joke going around that the Republicans are contemplating
changing their party symbol from an elephant to a snowball in
Hell. Funny.

Even if the perception is more or less true—even if the
Democrats are on the verge of establishing a Thousand Year
Reich—no one should expect to see the benefits trickle down to
the folks who most need them. With or without the Democrats,
people working in low-wage jobs will likely continue to be
victimized.

Not to pass judgment prematurely on the abilities of Labor
Secretary Hilda Solis or the commitment of the Obama
administration, but America's underclass is so far out of kilter,
so in need of recalibration, it will take a mammoth effort simply
to determine the scope of the problem.

Consider the recent findings by the Government Accountability
Office (GAO).

In a report issued on March 25, the GAO found that the Labor
Department's Wage and Hour Division (W&HD), the agency
charged with enforcing overtime and minimum wage provisions,
had egregiously mishandled several cases involving complaints
from low-wage workers. The report was the result of a "sting"
operation conducted by undercover federal agents posing as
workers.

The results were close to unbelievable. It's one thing for a
government bureaucracy to be inefficient and boorish; we've all
pretty much come to accept that. But it's quite another when a
help-the-underdog agency performs at near criminal levels of

ineptitude. According to a report published in the New York Times, the extent of the W&HD's dereliction was staggering.

One example: an agent posing as a dishwasher complained that he hadn't been paid the overtime wages due him for *almost five months*. The W&HD not only didn't return his call for several months, but when it did contact him, an agency official told him it would be another 8 to 10 months before they could get around to investigating the claim.

A minimum wage employee calls the Labor Department agency *specifically dedicated* to representing his interests, and the agency blows him off. It takes months to get back to the guy, and when they do get back, they tell him they won't be able to make the initial telephone inquiry for another 8 to 10 months. Unbelievable.

Another example: As part of the sting, a call was made to the W&HD reporting that under-age children in a northern California meat-packing plant were working during school hours, and being assigned to dangerous equipment. That tip should have raised a red flag. But what did the agency do? Nothing. They never responded, and the matter was never investigated. For all the W&HD knows, there's a whole crew of 11-year olds out there, making sausages.

During the GAO's investigation it was discovered that claims of *hundreds of thousands of dollars* in unpaid overtime (where employees were forced to work "off the clock") had never even been delved into. They had been totally ignored.

According to the GAO, the W&HD regularly abandoned cases when the employer didn't return its preliminary phone call, and in many instances the government official glibly advised the employee to "file a lawsuit" instead of relying on the agency for help. That has to win the Marie Antoinette Award for callousness: telling a minimum wage worker who's been gamed by his employer to go hire a lawyer.

It gets better.

During the nine-month sting operation, it was revealed that five of the ten "scripted" complaints were not even logged into the W&HD's official records; and in two other cases, the agency reported that the employees in question had been paid their back wages when, in fact, they had not. So not only did the agency not respond, they cooked the books.

The GAO found numerous instances of field agents being intimidated by employers, bending over backwards to accommodate management, and taking the employer's side against the employee, including allowing them to make restitution at pennies on the dollar. The report was a nightmare.

Secretary Solis has vowed to bolster the woefully undermanned agency by hiring an additional 250 investigators. That's a start. But the lesson here is that workers can't rely on government watchdogs; there are simply too many employees, too few dogs, and too many devious employers looking to swindle vulnerable workers.

With the government ruled out, and employees not having the necessary skills or muscle to do it themselves, that leaves only organized labor. If anybody ever needed a union to represent them, it's those vulnerable, low-wage workers who inhabit the economy's nether region.

Of course, now we know why the Chamber of Commerce fought so hard and spent so much money making sure the EFCA was shot down. Had universal card check become law, it might have been a whole new ballgame.

CounterPunch
2009

DE-SKILLING: AUTOMATION'S EVIL TWIN BROTHER

If there were any lingering doubts about Corporate America's contempt for working men and women, the on-going attempt to replace people with robots should put those doubts to rest. Clearly, a company that prefers a "mechanical man" to a functioning human being is trying to tell us something.

A recent announcement by Big Three automakers that they plan to invest a billion dollars over the next decade in the development of robotics reminded me of a remark made by an HR representative of the Kimberly-Clark Corporation, some years ago.

Off-handedly, he suggested that we might be surprised at what kind of workforce would, hypothetically, "scare" a management team. For example, it wouldn't be a lazy, belligerent or even militantly pro-union workforce. Those types, he assured us, could be "fixed" (his term). No, the scariest workforce would be a conspicuously talented one.

Why? Because talent is expensive. Talent is leverage. And while there is obviously a profound upside to having valuable workers, there is, paradoxically, a built-in downside: Management is now dependent upon a variable it can't control.

Typically, people with "careers" are interested in advancement, recognition, self-realization, etc. Ambition is recognized as a virtue and is encouraged. Conversely, people with "jobs" tend to focus on wages and benefits. But because wages and benefits constitute *overhead*, ambition among the "gravy-and-french fry crowd" (witty management-speak) is not only *discouraged,* it often needs to be "fixed."

Accordingly, management has embraced a strategy called "de-skilling," the systematic dumbing-down of jobs into easily mastered tasks. De-skilling is to virtuosity what Agent Orange is to foliage. While its primary goal is to improve efficiency through standardization, it's also a means of "neutralizing" a workforce.

We see a glimpse of it in the fast-food industry. Employees now press buttons with pictures of menu items. No arithmetic to mess with, no management worries about having enough cross-trained employees to go around. The job becomes, literally, as easy as A-B-C.

Warehousing is a better example. Before computerization, shipping checkers (the forklift drivers who load trucks) needed to know how to "cube out" a load. It was an art. They had to visualize the "cube," calculate its volume, number of cases, and number of stacks—to fill an 18-wheeler. It isn't rocket science, but it requires logic and finesse.

Today, the size and shape of every container in the warehouse—along with the interior dimensions of every trailer and boxcar in the yard—are logged into a computer. Everything is bar-coded. Monitors mounted on forklifts tell checkers where to go, what to scan, how much to grab, where to take it, and how to stack it.

While accuracy has improved significantly, productivity has not. Forcing checkers to paint by-the-numbers not only prevents any creative time-saving, it's a morale buster, an insult, like hitching a thoroughbred race horse to a plow. Also, with everything tied to one computer, a minor glitch now shuts down the entire warehouse.

But management got what they wanted. Checker-training used to require two months; now it's two weeks. Because experienced checkers were a relatively valuable commodity, they could earn $60,000 annually. Today, they compete with drivers making $11 an hour.

Companies tell unions not to worry. They remind them that automation Itself was once demonized, and that until workers saw the phenomenon in action and came to appreciate the advantages of mechanization, they feared it.

But automation arrived long before America's manufacturing sector had been hollowed-out and picked-over; it arrived when good jobs were still plentiful, and workers had time to adjust to new technology.

De-skilling is different. It has the potential to erode what's left of blue-collar dignity and leave in its wake a sub-class of drones. By stripping workers of their craft—effectively washing out their value on the open market—de-skilling has revealed itself as automation's evil twin brother. And there's no easy "fix" in sight.

CounterPunch
2007

FASCISM, INC.

Even though the term "fascist" is wildly overused and misapplied (usually intended to mean "authoritarian" or "totalitarian"), people who scoff at the analogy of Fascism to Corporationism, claiming the comparison is too goofy or insulting even to be dignified with a response, obviously haven't been paying attention.

What is Fascism? As delineated by Benito Mussolini himself (who, as a one-time journalist, coined the term), its chief features are: a charismatic leader, a near metaphysical sense of nationalism, a compulsion to dominate, and an appeal to symbols and myth. Fascism is confidence. Fascism is destiny. Expressed in the glib lingo of management consultants, Fascism is pro-active and Fascists are "winners."

Let's break it down.

Today's CEO—a hugely influential, lavishly compensated societal demi-god who's worshipped both inside and outside the hierarchy—is clearly analogous to Fascism's notion of a charismatic leader. Think about it. Who had more people drooling and gushing over him? General Electric's Jack Welsh, at the peak of GE's multi-billion dollar run, or Generalissimo Francisco Franco?

I knew of a low-level executive working for Boeing Corporation, in the 1990s, whose screen-saver was a photo of Boeing's CEO. No joke. This office minion actually chose to have the mug of the company CEO staring out at him from his computer. How is this different from a loyal Nazi hanging a portrait of Der Fuhrer on the wall?

As to a glorified sense of nationalism, surely that can be equated with the arrogant, unchallenged dominance corporations now command. Multi-national corporations not only monopolize the world's natural resources—just as colonial European powers once did—they imperiously dictate economic policy to governments and kings. Where classical Fascism's destiny was to gain geographical and cultural hegemony, corporate destiny is to "conquer" the world through its markets.

And as for symbolism and myth, consider management's motivational tools, their endless supply of slogans and buzzwords. Consider terms like paradigm shift, synergy-driven, adoption processes, base-tending, deferred success, blue-skying, workstream, time boxing, mission critical, disambiguate—along with dozens of other insipid, seminar-generated phrases that make you want to pull your teeth out.

Corporate mythologizing is multiplying like rabbits. An operations manager at my old facility had several—perhaps half a dozen—inspirational photos on his wall, one of which showed a group of cowboys herding cattle on a dusty prairie. The caption read: "In this world, you either make dust or eat dust."

This mid-level manager was a tough, plain-spoken, rough-around-the-edges ex-Marine who harbored delusions of becoming a company mandarin. While visiting with him on a union matter, I pointed to the wall and casually mentioned that I found his cowboy poster simple-minded and offensive. I was purposely antagonistic, hoping to provoke this man. Instead, he grinned as if I'd complimented him.

Another manager displayed a photo of a water skier knifing through the water behind a speedboat, with the caption, "In order to excel, sometimes you have to make waves." Call me a romantic, but this caption, along with that of the cowboy picture, brought to mind the German words, "Arbeit Macht Frei" (Work will set you free), the slogan posted at the entrance to Auschwitz.

One of the cool things about belonging to a union—and, in particular, being a union officer—is that you're not obligated to conform. Unlike those high achievers clinging to the corporate ladder, you don't have to believe or pretend to believe in all the happy horseshit being sent down the Human Resources pipeline. Because union people know they ain't going anywhere, they can regard it all with a jaundiced eye.

Management tried to hook organized labor, using flattery, bribes, threats, and appeals to cold, hard logic as the bait, but labor never bit—it never bought into that corporate culture deal, at least not when it still had the muscle and will to resist. Rather, unions operated within their own unique culture—a bare-boned, no-frills dedication to obtaining better wages, benefits and working conditions.

As to embracing the latest management jargon and seminar-speak, organized labor's view was simple: If you fast-trackers insist on using terms like "disincentivize" and "full optics" (i.e., a complete picture or overview of something) to express yourself, feel free, but don't expect us to copy you. You've got your shoptalk, we've got ours.

An anecdote: In 1997 I attended a management seminar to discuss, God help us, a topic called "Paradigm Busting." I found out later that the consultant who gave the presentation was paid $1,400 for six hours of "work." To the extent that most of what she offered was infantile, time-stalling exercises, this woman was a thief, and had she lived in Saudi Arabia, she would've been imprisoned.

There were about twenty-five people in the room, all management employees with the exception of myself and another union officer ("Joe") from the International. We spent the morning introducing ourselves (a nice time-filling device) and doing seminar stuff, then broke for lunch, reconvened, did some childish role-playing and brain-storming exercises in the afternoon. At the end of the session we all shared what we'd gained from the experience.

The consultant went around the room, starting at the right, and asked each one of us (another time-killing exercise) for our input. The chairs were arranged in an elongated horseshoe configuration and, as luck would have it, Joe and I occupied the last two seats on the left, which meant we spoke last.

Everyone gave glowing accounts of what they'd learned. While it's perfectly natural to try and points by kissing up to the bosses, some of their answers were nonethess quite nauseating.

112

When it was our turn, Joe and I were blunt, but not rude. After all, they were kind enough to invite us, and the sandwiches had been served on croissants rather than plain bread. The least we could do was be civil.

Still, there was no way two union goons were going to fib to these people, not about something as important as the future of the facility. We made it clear that, because this was a blue-collar enterprise, a paper mill—a bath and facial tissue manufacturing and converting facility—we felt the whole, gaudy exercise had been more or less a waste of time and money.

While we understood the importance of "attitude," we urged them to focus their resources specifically on the Big Three: increasing production, improving quality, reducing waste. Those problems concerned everyone, and, in our view, were solvable through newer technology, improved methodology, and better training, not through seminars or pep rallies.

Predictably, the consultant and company spokesperson's response to our criticism was polite but peevish. They thanked us for attending, restated their position, and announced that we were going to have to "agree to disagree." And that was it. The whole room glared at us as if we were obnoxious drunks at a wedding reception.

But in the corridor, outside earshot of the managers, a young engineer approached Joe and me and whispered, "I wish I had the freedom to say what you said. I totally agree with you. This stuff is bullshit." We thanked him for his candor. Casual and "unofficial" as his comment was, it nonetheless raised our spirits.

The bad news is that the subversive bastards finally got to us. The plant is now a hotbed of corporate culture. Even union members are walking around using words like "disincentivize." This wouldn't matter so much if working people were getting their fair share of the pie, but they're not; as management's wages and benefits continue to rise, the average workers' continue to fall.

113

While I don't have the "full optics" on it, there's no denying that the corporate monolith is continuing to grow, continuing to spread across the landscape. Fascism is definitely on the rise. Fascism is *winning*. Only they're now calling it Team Building.

THE MYTH OF THE "POWERFUL" TEACHERS UNION

"It is an ironic habit of human beings to run faster when we have lost our way."

—Rollo May

There's a myth circulating out there that not only threatens to ruin the reputation of America's school teachers, but has the potential to side-track any realistic hopes of education reform. It's the assertion that "powerful" teachers' unions are responsible for the decline of public education in the United States in general, and California in particular.

Propagators of this myth claim that the reason test scores of American children have sunk so low in recent years is because our public school teachers are too incompetent and lazy to provide adequate instruction.

Moreover, because the teachers' unions are so domineering and evil—because their leaders will do anything to maintain union hegemony, including not allowing demonstrably inferior teachers to be fired—school administrators are powerless to act.

You hear these charges everywhere. Arianna Huffington, the late-to-the-party liberal and celebrity blogger, has been echoing such claims for years. For Huffington to be riffing on the state of public education is, in itself, remarkable, given that she lives in Brentwood, her daughters attend prestigious private schools, and the closest she's ever come to an inner-city school was the day she accidentally drove by one, causing her to hastily lock the doors and windows of her Prius and speed away.

On Friday, March 13, comedian and uber-liberal Bill Maher joined the attack on his HBO show. In one of his signature tirades, Maher, a California resident, railed against the "powerful" California teachers' union, accusing it of contributing to the crisis in public education by not allowing the school district to remove incompetent teachers.

Maher came armed with statistics. He noted with dismay that the U.S. ranked 35th in the world in math, 29th in science, and that barely 50% of California's public school pupils manage to graduate from high school. He blamed the teachers for this.

Although every teacher in the LAUSD (Los Angeles Unified School District), has a college degree and a teaching credential and managed to survive the scrutiny of a lengthy probationary period, Maher piously maintained that these teachers were unqualified to run a classroom.

Granted, Maher is a professional comic trolling for laughs, and not a "social scientist" dispensing wisdom, so we shouldn't be looking to this man for enlightenment. Still, considering his liberal creds (from the environment to civil liberties to corporate mischief to drug law reform), it was demoralizing to hear someone this hip say something so stupid and simplistic.

Maher made a huge deal of the fact that, because of the union's protective shield, *less than 1%* of California's tenured/post-probationary teachers get fired. Although this ratio clearly outraged him (he appeared visibly upset by it), had he taken five minutes to research the subject, he'd have realized that this figure represents the national average—*with or without unions.*

In Georgia, where 92.5% of the teachers are non-union, only 0.5% of tenured/post-probationary teachers get fired. In South Carolina, where 100% of the teachers are non-union, it's 0.32%. And in North Carolina, where *97.7% are non-union*, a miniscule .03% of tenured/post-probationary teachers get fired—the *exact same percentage as California.*

An even more startling comparison: In California, with its "powerful" teachers' union, school administrators fire, on average, 6.91% of its probationary teachers. In non-union North Carolina, that figure is only 1.38%. California is actually *tougher* on prospective candidates.

So, despite Maher's display of civic pride and self-righteous indignation ("We need to *bust* this union," he declared), he was utterly mistaken. The statistics not only don't support his argument, they contradict it.

Fact: During the 1950s and 1960s, California's public school system was routinely ranked among the nation's finest. You can look it up. More significantly, the teachers in those classrooms were union members. The same teachers who were winning those awards for excellence belonged to the "powerful" teachers' union. Let that sink in a moment: Good schools, good teachers, big union.

Which raises the question: Has anything else changed in California (and the rest of the country, for that matter) in the last 40 years to lead one to believe there might be causes *other* than labor unions to explain the drop in graduation rates? Have there been any significant changes in, say, cultural attitudes or demographics?

For openers, how about the disintegration of the American family and the decline in parental supervision/involvement? Being a good student requires discipline, application and, perhaps, a certain level of respect for authority. Have we witnessed any "breakdowns" in these areas over the last 40 years?

Or how about the rise in urban poverty? Or the hollowing-out of the middle-class (the average worker hasn't received a pay increase, in *real dollars*, since 1973)? Or the assimilation of non-English-speaking immigrants? Or the decrease in per capita funding on California public education? Or the chaos created by school boards arbitrarily mandating wholesale changes in "educational ideology" every two years (LAUSD has spent hundreds of millions of dollars on consultants)?

Ask any teacher, child psychologist, sociologist, or real estate agent, and they'll tell you the same thing: As a general rule, good schools are found in good neighborhoods, and bad schools are found in bad neighborhoods. Simple as that.

Moreover, people know this "formula" to be true. Not only is the promise of good schools one reason why people with kids buy homes in good neighborhoods, it's not uncommon for parents in California to lie about their home addresses in order to get their children assigned to better schools.

An experiment: Try moving those "good" teachers from decent school districts—where the kids show up each day, on time, prepared, bright-eyed and attentive, having completed their homework, having eaten a nutritious breakfast, etc.—to one of those South Central LA shit-holes, where crime is rampant, neighborhoods are ravaged, families are in crisis, and 40% of the students live in foster care.

See if these "good" teachers, by virtue of their innate "classroom abilities," are able to improve the test scores of these stunted, overmatched and underprivileged kids. See if these "good" teachers can do what a generation of parents themselves, and society itself, can't seem to do; see if the graduation rates in these depressed communities rise significantly.

And, as part of that same experiment, move the "incompetent" teachers to these healthy, self-sustaining districts and see if the students in these schools don't continue to score significantly higher, even with the "bad" teachers now running the show.

Fact: Oregon has a good public school system. So do South Dakota, Vermont, Connecticut, Wisconsin, Minnesota, Maine and Washington, among others. Is that because the folks living in these states are exceptionally bright? Is it because their teachers are extraordinarily talented?

Or is it because these school districts are stable, relatively homogeneous, and don't face a fraction of the challenges facing California?

For the record, the teachers in these aforementioned good schools are overwhelmingly unionized. Oregon and Washington teachers are 100% unionized; Wisconsin is 98%; Connecticut is 98%; etc.

118

Also, comparing the scores of American students in foreign countries is a bit misleading. The United States was not only the first nation in the world to offer free public education, it was the first to make it compulsory.

In the U.S., by law, you must attend school until at least age 16 (some states have even higher age requirements). That means our national average is going to incorporate test scores of every kid from every background in every neighborhood in the country.

In India (where I once lived and worked), great emphasis is placed on education; accordingly, India has a decent school system, one that scores well. But school attendance is *not mandatory*. Indeed, India has 400 million people who are *illiterate*. One wonders what their national test scores would be if those many millions who can't read or write were factored in.

Fact: Teachers *can* be fired. Who honestly believes a teachers' union—whether in California, Oregon or Connecticut—has the authority to insist that management keep unqualified teachers? Since when does a labor union *dictate* to management? Since when does the hired help tell the bosses what to do? The accusation is absurd on its face.

Fact: During the *first two years* of employment, any teacher in the LAUSD can be fired for any reason, with no recourse to union representation and no access to the grievance procedure. Two full years. If the district doesn't like you for any reason, they fire you. No union. No grievance. Nothing. Could any arrangement be more favorable to management?

Yet, the myth persists, the myth of the Unqualified Teacher. Instead of identifying the *real* problems facing California's schools (daunting as they may be), and trying to solve them, people stubbornly insist that *thousands* of our teachers—every one of them college-educated, credentialed, and having survived two years of scrutiny—need to be fired.

Let's be clear; no one is suggesting that all teachers are "excellent." Obviously, you're going to find marginal workers in any profession. But, realistically, how many "bad" teachers could there be?

Surely, America's colleges, universities, and credentialing system can't be so hideously flawed that we no longer trust their output—that our teachers aren't worth a damn. Moreover, if it's the unions who are protecting them, why does South Carolina—where 100% of the teachers are non-union—fire only *one-third of one-percent* of them?

Fact: The fault for unqualified teachers remaining on the payroll lies entirely with the school administrators. These overpaid, $120,000 a year, gutless bureaucrats want us to believe that we live in a world turned upside down. A world where, fantastically, the bosses answer to the employees.

Arguably, the problems facing America's public schools are staggering. But because politicians are essentially spineless—fearful of doing or saying anything that would risk antagonizing their "base"—they refuse to address the *real* issues. Instead, they play little mind games with the voters. It's not a pretty picture, but it's where we stand.

And if television personalities like Arianna Huffington and Bill Maher honestly believe all this anti-union propaganda being circulated, they're much more gullible than we thought.

CounterPunch
2009

LOOKING FOR MR. LOOPHOLE

"Capitalism is the extraordinary belief that the nastiest of men, for the nastiest of reasons, will somehow work for the benefit of us all."

—John Maynard Keynes

How far-fetched and audacious would it be to assign the title of "senior vice-president of dough-making" to an hourly employee at a bakery, in order to avoid having to pay his Workers Compensation premiums? As an "executive" in the company and one of its sole equity partners, this employee would be exempted by law.

Far-fetched or not, it happened. The ploy was used by Pic-A-Bagel, a San Diego novelty food company. While the Workers Compensation Appeals Board rightly concluded that the job designation was fictitious, Pic-A-Bagel's insurance underwriters shamelessly challenged the decision and took it to court. Happily, the 4th District Court of Appeal ruled against them.

On February 25, 2009, California's Attorney General, Jerry Brown, took steps to stop a similar ploy. Contractors Asset Protection Association Inc. (Contractors APA), a Rancho Santa Fe corporation, makes its living by counseling small companies on how to avoid paying Workers Comp premiums for their employees.

Contractors APA is accused of advising its clients to re-classify their hourly and salaried employees as "corporate officers" and "sole share-holders" in the company as a means of withholding premiums. Clients were assured that, even with the bogus "paper" titles and share-holdings, there was no way these employees could do any corporate mischief. Recognizing the practice for the naked, money-grubbing scam it was, the State of California filed a lawsuit seeking a permanent injunction and a minimum of $300,000 in penalties.

Workers Compensation has been on the books for almost a century. Briefly, it is the system by which employees who are injured on the job receive, among other benefits, partial reimbursement for lost wages, free medical expenses to treat the injury, and lump-sum compensation if permanently disabled. The fund is financed by employers who make regular monthly contributions, and the settlements are generally handled by private insurance companies in conjunction with the state Workers Compensation Board.

Given that Workers Compensation premiums can be expensive, why were America's businesses so willing to agree to something that would cost them additional money? The answer is simple: It made good, long-term business sense. Workers Comp requires injured workers to relinquish their right to sue their employer for the "tort of negligence."

In other words, when a worker gets hurt on the job—even if the injury results in a permanent disability or death—the company cannot be sued for negligence. Also, there are no punitive damages attached to Workers Comp, and no compensation for pain or suffering. While companies have, over time, come to view Workers Comp as a form of "insurance," one that indemnifies them against potentially crippling lawsuits, employees see it as a prompt, low-hassle means of being reimbursed for work-related injuries. It was a trade-off for both sides.

Begun originally in Europe, the first Workers Compensation statutes in the U.S. went into effect in 1911, in Wisconsin. By 1949, every state in the union had some form of it. For working people, one of the great benefits of Workers Comp—besides the lost wages and medical care—was that it demonstrably improved the safety conditions at industrial job sites in the United States. To avoid having to pay for injuries, companies finally took seriously the need to make jobs safer.

The outrageous (and illegal) attempts by Pic-A-Bagel and Contractors APA to find loopholes in the Workers Comp system bring to mind another fairly recent management scam to avoid additional costs—the so-called Kentucky River Decision. Unfortunately, this maneuver was not only determined *not* to be illegal, it was adopted as the law of the land.

This case involved nurses and other health care workers being re-classified as "supervisors" by their employers in order to exempt them from joining a labor union. Previously these workers were classified under the labor code as "crew leaders" or (to use an anachronistic term) "straw bosses," designations that allowed them to perform certain leadership tasks (without anything approaching the authority of an actual "supervisor"), while still entitled to seek union representation.

But the Bush administration's NLRB (National Labor Relations Board), under pressure from anti-union business groups across the country, overruled these time-honored distinctions, and declared that "leads" and "charge nurses" were now classified as "supervisory" employees and, therefore, under the statutes of federal labor law, were exempt from joining a labor union.

This slick maneuver, which instantly affected thousands of health care employees, stands as one more example of just how defiantly anti-union the Elaine Chao (Bush's Secretary of Labor) regime was. Her two terms as Secretary resulted in an uphill battle and eight years of bad news for organized labor.

Attorney General Brown's decision to take action against the Workers Comp swindlers in California was obviously a step in the right direction. Now what we need to see is Hilda Solis (the recently confirmed Secretary of Labor) move to have that dreadful Kentucky River Decision overturned.

The Exception Magazine
2009

THE UNBEARABLE LIGHTNESS OF UNION MEMBERSHIP

"Perhaps the rare and simple pleasure of being seen for what one is compensates for the misery of being it."
—Margaret Drabble

It's astonishing, really, how quickly things can shift in the national consciousness, how effortlessly something can go from being considered outrageous or fantastic to being treated as unremarkable or mundane.

For example, everybody and his brother is now bandying about the word "billion" as if it were merely a "thousand" on steroids. A billion dollars is now a figure which ordinary tax-payers (those earning a modest $50,000-$70,000 a year) are expected to wrap their minds around while drinking their morning coffee. Clearly, the number has lost its shock value.

It's discouraging that people who regularly clip coupons—the same folks who went berserk when gasoline reached $4.00 a gallon—are the same tax-payers who yawned when they learned of the recent bailout. "Hey, did you hear the feds are going to spend $700 billion to help the banks!?" "Yeah, whatever."

But a billion dollars is a shit-load of money. Consider: If a person were given a *million* dollars and told to spend $1,000 a day until he ran out of money, he'd run out of money in about 3 years. If he were given a *billion* dollars and told to spend $1,000 a day, he'd run out of money in about 3,000 years.

Because a billion dollars is a staggering, almost incomprehensible sum, it should elicit a profound sense of caution and unease when politicians contemplate spending it. But it doesn't. It's lost its potency. And now, of course, financial analysts are blithely talking about a *trillion* dollars— which is a thousand billion—as if the very fact that the word rolls so smoothly off their tongues makes it somehow less preposterous.

Another bit of goofy conventional wisdom that's been reinforced by a lack of examination is the notion that America's loss of jobs, loss of key industries, and loss of its once-mighty manufacturing base, is, at root, the result of America's labor force not being competent or committed enough to keep itself in the game.

Although politicians still pay lip service, patriotically referring to the American worker as "the best damn worker in the world," there's an undercurrent of skepticism, a nagging belief that, perhaps, the American worker has gotten too complacent, become too soft, and that foreign workers are simply "hungrier" than we are. The American worker has come under scrutiny. And no sector of the workforce has received more of the stink-eye than union members.

Here's a true story, a union story, that happened some years ago in the Materials Handling department of the Kimberly-Clark Corporation's Fullerton, California, paper mill. Arguably, it's emblematic of what takes place in work sites all over the country. To fully appreciate it, a little background is required.

Like hundreds of other companies during the 1990s, Kimberly-Clark was eagerly exploring ways to maximize its profits by downsizing its workforce. The mantra of the day for American businesses, from government jobs to private industry to academic institutions, was "Lower the headcount." Companies gleefully rubbed their hands together at the prospect of slashing their unit-labor costs by decimating the workforce, ushering in that other, equally obnoxious mantra: "More with less."

Because the Kimberly-Clark plant had already lost approximately 30% of its workers—both salaried and hourly—through layoffs, buyouts and natural attrition, everyone except the most senior employees in the facility were understandably nervous. Equally demoralizing, with the work environment now so hostile and toxic, no one was having any fun on their jobs; and if you can't have any fun on your job (unless you're busy saving lives in the ER of a big city hospital), you've chosen the wrong line of work.

Encouraged by the union's concessionary posture, and interpreting its willingness to join the "team" (e.g., participate in management team-building seminars) as evidence of weakness, the company was now taking previously inconceivable liberties. Not only had they become arrogant and demanding, they had turned into virtual bullies.

There was a new sheriff in town. Coffee breaks were shortened; restroom breaks were now being "timed" (by computer); people were hounded for minor infractions; safety was subordinated to production goals; and people were putting in a ridiculous number of hours (And why not? They were being asked to do an exorbitant amount of work.). It was the Chinese Year of the Pissant.

And no one in the facility was having less fun than the Materials Handling department. The MH warehouse was where all the paper products manufactured by Kimberly-Clark (Huggie diapers, Kleenex, Kotex, Scott Towels, etc.) were loaded on to trucks and shipped to retail and wholesale outlets across the United States. Having heard for years (decades, really) predictions of its imminent demise, the Materials Handling guys were finally starting to believe those rumors, and it was putting the zap on their heads.

After all, warehouses throughout the industry were being shutdown, co-opted or run by skeleton crews. All one had to do was look around and see the writing on the wall. Radically scaling back the operation of Fullerton's 1,000,000 square foot warehouse seemed to make sense, especially considering that union forklift drivers were earning $20 per hour, and could be replaced by satellite warehouse drivers earning barely half that rate.

To put the skids to this runaway, lower-the-headcount-at-any-cost mentality, and stop the company from treating its employees like plantation slaves, one of the union's shop stewards suggested resorting to a time-honored device—one that goes all the way back to the late 19th century—known as the "work to rule" strategy.

Used originally by miners and early textile workers to resist being worked to death, the strategy consisted of getting all the hourly employees to do *precisely* what their job descriptions specified—no more, no less—and, most importantly, to follow the department safety manual to the letter.

The idea was to get the company to back off, to force management to abandon its downsizing frenzy by having the workforce demonstrate that more people were required to get the jobs done than the company was scheduling, and to get them to recognize that workers weren't going to stand idly by and watch their numbers dwindle while management systematically dehumanized them.

The work-to-rule strategy was originally adopted because it was infinitely less aggressive (and risky) than going on strike. As a "legal" form of worker disobedience, it made eminent sense.

Despite what some people believe about union members, the overwhelming majority of them not only want to perform their jobs with distinction, they want management to acknowledge that performance. Call it "needy" or "insecure" or whatever, but people want to be acknowledged as valuable employees. And that pride in being acknowledged as good workers turned out to be the fly in the ointment.

Kimberly-Clark's warehouse drivers had not only gotten into the habit of straining to surpass their shipping quotas (even though those quotas had already been significantly raised, and that extra effort had resulted in zero additional compensation) but, alarmingly, they'd also taken to ignoring many of the safety regulations laid out in the department safety manual. They were taking shortcuts.

Employee safety was, in principle, a huge concern to the company. Any driver observed violating a vehicle safety rule was subject to a formal reprimand; moreover, any driver who continued violating written safety rules was subject to discharge. While safety write-ups were rare, they weren't unheard of. Therefore, getting the department's crews to join in the "safety slowdown" had a legal and defensible basis.

But here's the punchline. Even in the face of arduous, increasingly demanding workloads which, as a matter of simple arithmetic, could eventually lead to people working themselves right out of a job, the crews refused to join in the coordinated slowdown. The department shop stewards who fanned out among the crews and tried to foment this minor "mutiny" couldn't get any takers. In fact, many employees reacted angrily to the suggestion that they purposely work "less hard."

This response was not the result of fear of company retaliation. In addition to being assured by union leadership that so long as they didn't cross the line from "slow and steady" to outright "insubordination" they were totally within their rights to work at a more relaxed pace, these drivers were some of the toughest union members in the plant. Indeed, the Materials Handling department was famously prickly and recalcitrant, regularly leading the plant in management-union confrontations and in the number of formal grievances filed by the union.

But as hard-nosed and confrontational as they were, the crews drew the line at "disgracing" themselves as workers. As angry and disillusioned with the company as they were, they still had enormous pride in their work. And that's what caused the Local's attempt at a grassroots revolt to fail.

It was downright embarrassing. We were supposed to be this bad-ass labor union, and yet we couldn't get our own members to join in a little rebellious mischief? Even when that mischief was clearly in their best interest? But they wouldn't go for it— not if it risked making them look like deadbeats.

In truth, I would argue that this snapshot is more or less representative of union workers everywhere. Because union jobs generally offer significantly better working conditions, wages and benefits than non-union jobs, these jobs attract a higher caliber worker. It makes sense. The better the job perks, the better worker they're going to attract.

Given what's happened to the country—with jobs being shipped abroad and workers being increasingly isolated and dehumanized—it's hard to imagine how working people manage to stay with it, how they continue to hang in there. Seeing the way patriotic workers have been so grossly disrespected by Corporate America is enough to break your heart. Break it into a million pieces. A billion pieces.

CounterPunch
2008

A LOOK AT THE EMPLOYEE FREE CHOICE ACT

By now, most people have heard of the Employee Free Choice Act (EFCA), the bold legislative initiative introduced by the Democrats (Rep. George Miller, D-CA), intended to amend the National Labor Relations Act (NLRA) by making it easier and fairer for employees to join a labor union.

Although the measure passed the House by a vote of 241 to 185, in June of 2007, and was approved by a 51-48 vote in the Senate, it failed to get the 60 votes necessary for cloture (which would have made it filibuster-proof), causing it to lie dormant for the remainder of the 110th Congress.

However, it should be noted that President Bush had already promised to veto the legislation, so even with those 60 crucial Senate votes the bill would have emerged stillborn. To have any chance whatever of becoming law, it was clear that the EFCA would require a Democrat in the White House.

During the primaries, both Obama and Clinton loudly sang the praises of the EFCA (as they raked in organized labor's contributions) and promised, if elected, to fight for its passage. But because there have been signs that President Obama is hedging on that promise, it remains to be seen how hard he and his Congress-savvy chief of staff Rahm Emanuel will push for it. On one side, they have moderate Democrats terrified of provoking the Republicans; on the other, they have an aroused AFL-CIO applying pressure.

If enacted, EFCA would allow employees to circumvent the complex, time-consuming, and management-skewed NLRB certification process. Instead of a full-blown election, workers would have the choice of "card check," where all they have to do is sign cards indicating they wish to become union members. If a majority of the workforce signs such cards they instantly belong to a union.

Naturally, most businesses hate the idea of the streamlining the process. They object to anything that makes joining a union easier. Indeed, if it were their call, many businesses would prefer seeing unions made illegal or "state-run," as they are in the most repressive countries in the world. Accordingly, the U.S. Chamber of Commerce has spent millions lobbying against passage of the EFCA.

While card check is the most celebrated feature of the EFCA, there are two other provisions in this bill that are equally—if not *more*—important. Card check is an enormous advantage to unions, but it's not a "new" method. It's already used voluntarily by companies who feel they can either defeat the measure through anti-union propaganda, or believe there's benefit in being seen as "labor friendly."

But the two other features of this bill could be seen as labor milestones.

First, the EFCA will give the union the right to demand that the company begin contract negotiations *within 10 days* of certification. Ask any union organizers how hard it is to get that first contract, and they'll tell you that companies are notorious for dragging their feet—either by stalling interminably before sitting down with the union, or purposely prolonging the negotiations to the point where novice memberships get so antsy, they lose their nerve and ask for decertification. It happens.

However, under the EFCA, if the parties are unable to reach an agreement *within 90 days,* either side, union or management, can request that the Federal Mediation and Conciliation Service (FMCS) be brought in to mediate the bargain. Mediators already assist in contract bargains, particularly when strikes have been called or appear to be imminent, so having one present isn't innovative.

But here's the astonishing part: If the parties can't reach a mediated settlement *within 30 days*, the FMCS has the authority to finalize the contract. In effect, it would be binding arbitration. The notion of an outside party—a government agency, no less—setting the terms of a labor agreement would put the fear of God in management, causing them to do everything in their power to reach an equitable agreement. It's a profound improvement to the process.

Second, the EFCA would require the NLRB to seek an immediate injunction when there is "reasonable cause" to believe an employer has fired, suspended or harassed an employee for engaging in a union organizing or first contract drive. Moreover, an employer who is found guilty of illegally firing or suspending a union activist would be required to pay that employee *three times his back pay*—the amount of his lost wages, plus two times that sum in punitive damages—plus as much as $20,000 in civil fines.

So there it is. The EFCA will not only make card check a way of life, it will prevent companies who hope to avoid having to agree to a fair contract from stalling or playing mind games at the bargaining table, and will stop (or seriously curtail) management from illegally thwarting union activism in the workplace.

It's no wonder the Republican Party and the U.S. Chamber of Commerce are going ape-shit over this. Arguably, the EFCA would be the first big-time pro-labor legislation to come down the pike since the 1935 Wagner Act. Now it's up to Obama and the Democrats to step up to the plate and get it done.

CounterPunch
2009

COPS AND LABOR UNIONS

"If anyone has been offended, I'm sorry for that."
—LA Chief of Police Darryl F. Gates
(in response to being criticized for suggesting that more blacks than whites die from police chokeholds because their carotid arteries "do not open as fast as normal people." LA Times, May 11, 1982.)

The Henry Louis Gates confrontation with the Cambridge police department, back in July, was a dramatic reminder that virtually every citizen has an anecdote or two involving the police—either how the cops rousted, annoyed, or otherwise disrespected them, or, conversely, how the police helped them or let them off the hook.

Like most people, my own experiences are mixed. I've been generously allowed to slide on traffic violations, and I've been arbitrarily ticketed for what I considered marginal, nitpicking offenses. As a college student I engaged in some stupid pranks which, had the police chosen to arrest us instead of scolding us, would have put me in front of a judge, if not in a jail cell.

But even with these discrepancies and inconsistencies, unlike African-Americans, Hispanics or the poor, I've never felt that my treatment had anything to do with my ethnicity or socio-economic status. Good cop-bad cop, nice cop-mean cop, understanding cop-stubborn cop—none of it had to do with my status as a human being.

And while, like most people, I object to the way the police routinely treat the homeless and underclass—and, as a former union rep, can't forget the treasonous role law enforcement played in organized labor's struggle, serving as management goon squads and strike-breakers—I also realize the police reflect the values of society at large.

To the extent that we're a race of shameless snobs and celebrity hounds, we can expect cops to bully the weakest and least prepossessing among us, and gush over the richest and most glamorous. Cops are no different than the rest of the herd. Except they carry a badge and a gun and have the authority (along with the burning desire) to detain, imprison, or kill us, which, unfortunately, makes all the difference in the world.

I've probably known more police than the average person, and more than I've actually wanted to know. There was a saloon near the union hall which cops regularly patronized, and I had a friend who was an officer with the LA County Sheriff's Department, who delighted in educating naïve little me on "real life" police practices.

While none of his stories could be described as "shocking," it was unsettling to hear them presented as standard procedure. For instance, he said that cops make a practice of "tuning up" anyone who tries to run away from them. "When we tell you to stop," he said, "you'd better stop. If you make us chase you, you're going to pay for it." When I reminded him that it was illegal for cops to beat up their prisoners, he just rolled his eyes.

He also told me that when they spot a car on the road at 2:30 a.m. with black men in it, they will automatically pull it over, using some phony reason, such as an improper lane change or faulty tail light, as an excuse.

Why would you stop a car with black guys in it when there's no violation? "Because there are black guys in it," he deadpanned. He was neither apologetic nor embarrassed at admitting to racial profiling because he honestly believed stopping a car full of black men at 2:30 a.m. is what any conscientious police officer would do.

Surprisingly, when you talk to the police about their union you find that most of them (unlike industrial union members) have a fairly high opinion of it. Part of that is because cops don't trust anyone except other cops, and they realize that, as imperfect and "political" (their most common criticism) as their union may be, it's nonetheless composed of nothing but cops, former cops, and cop lawyers.

While that "us vs. them" mentality—the notion that there is a Thin Blue Line separating civilization from the jungle—may be beneficial in maintaining a sense of camaraderie, it's also a breeding ground for fanaticism and self-deception. Even though, statistically, 98% of the population are law-abiding citizens, cops tend to approach most of us as if we belong to that 2%.

And of course, that whole celebrity jock-sniffer dynamic is magnified exponentially when it involves conspicuous wealth and prestige. The police can deny it all they like, but cops behave differently when they ring the doorbell of an ostentatious mansion, and when they pound on the door of some beat-up woodframe house in the inner city.

Just think how marvelous it would be if the opposite occurred—if the police had the moral courage to display even the barest trace of egalitarian defiance by treating the very wealthy with a minimum of civility and the demonstrably poor with a profound sense of respect.

Still, even given these inherent prejudices, a willingness to play the game can get you out of a jam. Arguably, you shouldn't have to act all deferential and courteous in order to catch a break; you shouldn't have to kiss up to them. After all, these are cops, civil servants, not noblemen. But if you want to avoid trouble (as any young black man can tell you), it's often wise to be as humble as a supplicant.

During a strike some years ago, several of our union members were involved in minor brushes with the police—most having to do with disturbances on the picket lines, most occurring during the midnight shift, and, alas, most having to do with alcohol.

Based on reports I received from witnesses, the police were astonishingly reserved in their responses. For example, when alcohol was involved, the cops did little more than caution the drinkers not to make total asses of themselves and not to get behind the wheel of a car; and when there was a skirmish or physical confrontation, they managed to settle it without arresting anyone.

However, it must be emphasized that, according to these same witnesses, because most of these picketers happened to be fairly savvy in the ways of the world, they were careful not to violate the cardinal rule of citizen-police interaction: Thou Shall Not Sass. And it worked.

Granted, these union incidents occurred in conservative Orange County, California. The cops were white and none of the picketers were African-American. Had the drinkers and rowdies on the picket line been young black men, things might have played out differently.

The Exception Magazine
2009

WHEN EMPLOYEES ARE FIRED ILLEGALLY

Despite the recent banking debacle, Free Market fundamentalists remain opposed to burdening our financial institutions with more strident regulations and safeguards, arguing that it's not the paucity of regulations that's the problem (we've already got enough laws on the books, they argue), but the people who willfully violate them. Warn everyone that this time we really mean business, and the problem will go away.

The same argument is used by opponents of the EFCA (Employee Free Choice Act), whose provisions include additional penalties for companies found guilty of harassing, intimidating or terminating employees engaged in union activism. Its opponents argue that there are already ULP (unfair labor practice) statutes on the books making these practices illegal. Why clog the system with more laws? Instead, why not enforce the ones we already have?

While this all sounds perfectly reasonable in theory, in truth, current labor laws are not only woefully ambiguous, they are under-enforced to the point of negligence. And they will remain under-enforced until they've been reinvigorated and recast, injected with new life, placed in the hands of new enforcers, and given sharper teeth.

Just as gluttonous Wall Street bankers would love to be slapped on the wrist and allowed to go back to their financial high-wire act (with government safety nets available in case they fall down), Corporate America would love to see federal labor laws remain just the way they are—vague, hazy and more or less ignored.

The intimidation and harassment of employees engaged in union activism is a major reason why membership in the U.S. remains at a puny 12.4%—despite polls indicating that as many as 60% of America's workers have expressed interest in joining a union. Working people are understandably scared. Terrified of losing their job or being harassed to death, they're unwilling to have their pro-union sentiments made public.

Wal-Mart employees tell horror stories of being "interrogated" by company officials who suspect them of having met with a union organizer in the parking lot (surveillance cameras monitor the premises) and not reporting it. So hysterical is Wal-Mart's fear of labor unions, workers are not only regularly subjected to virulent, anti-union propaganda sessions, they're reminded that they're *required to report* any attempt by a union organizer to pass out literature or engage them in a conversation about unions.

If the stakes weren't so high, and the situation didn't have such dreadful implications, these startling accounts—of Wal-Mart managers behaving like concerned parents, warning their children to report any strange man who tries to give them candy—would be morbidly funny.

As conspicuous as Wal-Mart is, it isn't the only vehemently anti-union company out there; indeed, there are hundreds more just as vehement. But given the mega-retailer's gluttonous scope and influence, it has come to be regarded as the Grand Mikado of anti-union propagandists. And, in contrast to a typical hard-nosed company, where the ends often *justify* the means; at Wal-Mart, alas, the ends *sanctify* the means.

Of course, if a company wants to bombard its workers with anti-union venom, that's their right. After all, it's their enterprise, their investment, their property, blah, blah, blah. But harassing or firing an employee for distributing union literature is a whole other deal. Specifically, it's illegal. One can think of a business as his own private domain all he likes, but harassing pro-union employees is against the law. They find you guilty, they punish you.

A non-union worker is, by definition, outmanned and outgunned. Facing a multi-billion dollar conglomerate by himself, he has about as much chance of "winning" as a one-armed pissant against a steamroller. When a non-union worker gets fired for engaging in union activism, he has no one to represent him. Because he doesn't belong to a union—despite his best efforts to join one—he has limited access to the legal apparatus.

Yes, federal laws permit you to challenge your discharge with the NLRB; and, yes, the union you're seeking to affiliate with will usually provide assistance. But unlawful termination cases—even those adjudicated by sympathetic NLRB panels (of which there were few under Bush's Secretary of Labor, Elaine Chao)—are notoriously difficult to prove. In truth, the overwhelming majority of these petitioners lose their appeals. And, unless you're part of a big-time, national organizing drive, it's unlikely your prospective union will push the case as far as it can go.

Moreover, these reinstatement hearings can take as long as a year or two to resolve. Even if you win back your job, you can pretty much kiss off any union organizing drive because—besides scaring the bejeezus out of your fellow workers (who, having seen you get fired, slinked back into the shadows)—whatever momentum there was has long since fizzled out. Timing is everything. The moment has come and gone.

It goes without saying that companies are not only aware of this dynamic, they rejoice in exploiting it. They behave like your typical "bully." The same management team who is tentative, even reluctant, about butting heads with a big, bad labor union, can be downright ruthless and cavalier when it comes to getting rid of a vulnerable "unrepresented" union agitator.

So it's a Catch 22 dilemma. You can't get the full representation you need without belonging to a union. But you can't belong to a union if you don't have a job—not even if you had a job and were *illegally* fired from it for trying to gain access to a union (which would have represented you, had you belonged to it).

Meanwhile, Wal-Mart remains a defiantly non-union employer. It continues to prosper. It continues to grow, further cementing its status as the largest retailer in history. It continues to promote its corporate slogan: "Save money. Live better."

A few years ago, SEIU (Service Employees International Union) president Andy Stern flew to China as a guest of Lee Scott (CEO of Wal-Mart), presumably to get a firsthand look at the most infamous, government-controlled lapdog union in the world—the ACFTU (All China Federation of Trade Unions). Ain't that a kick in the head?

CounterPunch
2009

SIX WAYS TO REVIVE THE LABOR MOVEMENT

> "Fools make feasts, and wise folk eat them; the wise
> make jests, and the fools repeat them."
> —Gaelic proverb

If America's working people are going to make any meaningful progress, they'll need something more promising than having the recession end. After all, they were disadvantaged before the recession hit (during the so-called "boom" years), and, unless things change, they're certain to remain disadvantaged after we climb out of it.

Because the government can't or won't do it, and because management will never voluntarily give employees one dime more than it absolutely has to, it's up to organized labor to lead the charge. Unfortunately (and for a multitude of reasons), it's been a while since labor has been a significant factor in the economy.

Here are six ways unions can help themselves.

First, promote your history. Remembering who they are and where they came from should be as important to union people as remembering what happened at Iwo Jima is to the U.S. Marine Corps. America loves a scrappy fighter, particularly a scrappy underdog; and the labor movement is nothing if not an underdog.

The movement wasn't invented by academics or social do-gooders or political action committees; it wasn't the product of legislation. It originated in our streets, warehouses, factories and mines, and, corny as it sounds, was forged in sacrifice and bloodshed.

While no one's advocating a return to violence, labor must take a deep breath, and ask itself what it wants to be when it grows up—the loyal opposition or Corporate America's favorite sidekick? One suggestion? Lose that "buttoned-down" persona, where union leaders try to mimic the polished rhetoric and

general worminess of business executives. It ain't becoming.
Let Harry Bridges be your role model, not Michael Eisner.

Second, if potential union members consist of those hard-
working, gun-toting, Red State patriots who refuse to join
because they think workers' collectives are "un-American," then
wrap yourself in the flag. Expose the Ruling Class for what it is:
greedy, anti-patriotic bastards who care more about making
money than improving the country.

If the appeal to patriotism can motivate these folks, then
remind them that they're far more apt to find genuine "patriots"
on Main Street than on Wall Street. In 1980, the top 1% of
America's richest citizens owned 9% of the wealth. By 2007
that figure had jumped to 21%. During the same period,
average wages (in adjusted dollars) *declined*. Organized labor
needs to drive home that Us vs. Them dynamic.

Third, don't shrink away from ideology. When critics scream
that such a divisive approach is an invitation to class warfare
and a veiled call for the redistribution of wealth, labor must
stand tall. Instead of apologetically denying such "radical"
accusations (which, alas, has been labor's recent history), it
needs to throw down the gauntlet and answer unequivocally,
"Yes, that's exactly what it is."

Fourth, rethink your political strategy. Flattery and
solicitousness don't work. President Obama found that out
when he invited key Republicans to watch the Super Bowl at the
White House, hoping they'd return the favor by embracing his
health care and banking reform programs.

God help us, even bribes don't work. Since the 1930s, labor has
contributed hundreds of millions of dollars to the Democrats.
Arguably, if even a *dime* on every dollar had come back as a
labor-friendly gesture, union membership would be at the 35%
rate it was in the early 1950s, instead of the 12.4% it is today.
Because the Democrats have failed the movement, labor needs
to choke them off.

Fifth, remind people that the most prosperous period in our history was when union membership was at its peak. Remind them that without a viable middle-class we won't have enough consumers left to do the consuming. Remind them that without a middle-class we risk being reduced to a bloated Third World financial services entity—part-Zurich, part-Bangladesh.

Also, drum home the fact that America's enemies—those "evil" countries around the world we've been taught to fear—all have one thing in common: independent labor unions are illegal. They're outlawed.

And sixth, demand more of the rank-and-file. For too long organized labor has coddled its membership. Obsessed with the drop in national membership rolls, worried that union members will run away, and terrified of being voted out of office, labor's leaders have failed to challenge the membership. That has to change.

Unions need to start requiring members to get involved. Just as shop stewards are given rebates on monthly dues, rank-and-file members should get a similar deal, in the form of dues credits for carrying out labor-oriented community service.

There are 16.1 million union members in the U.S. That represents an under-utilized, virtually untapped source of goodwill. If they conducted themselves as labor's emissaries or ambassadors, it could make an enormous difference.

And don't say it's too late; don't say labor can't turn the corner and once again become a powerful economic force. Things can change in an instant. Two months ago, who would've predicted there'd be half a million Iranians protesting in the streets?

CounterPunch
2009

HOW WE SPEND OUR MONEY

"Clothes make the poor invisible. America has the best-dressed poverty the world has ever known."
—Michael Harrington

In about three weeks (on July 24), the federal minimum wage will be raised 70-cents, from $6.55 to $7.25. At the new rate, if you work 40 hours a week, 52 weeks a year, and never miss a day, your annual gross will be $15,059. That's before any deductions, and assuming you can land a full-time, 40-hour a week job.

I used to live in India, back when it was still a "poor" country. I'm being facetious, of course. Despite what we hear about all those U.S. jobs being shipped over there, and the prodigious wealth of tycoons like Ratan Tata, president of the Tata Steel conglomerate, India remains a crushingly poor country.

While there's been enormous economic growth over the last three decades, India, with a population of just under 1.1 billion, still has *hundreds of millions* of illiterate people condemned to subsistence-level poverty. Malnutrition haunts the subcontinent, infant mortality is high, and universal rural electrification is still a fantasy.

And because India is a poor country, it behaves like a poor country. Unlike America, where poor people make the lifestyle choice of "pretending" not to be poor, Indians don't have that luxury. For that matter, neither do the underclass Mexicans living and working in the U.S.—those who wash our dishes, scrub our floors and pick our fruit. They don't lease new cars or dress beyond their means. That's more or less an American story.

Poor Indians are easy to identify because they don't step outside themselves. A poor Indian would never think of saving up to buy $90 running shoes or splurging on a rented limo, to see how it feels to live large. At Indian markets you can buy a single egg or single cigarette, because people can't afford full cartons or packs.

By contrast, it's *amazing* how we Americans spend our money. The same conscientious consumer who's willing to drive five miles out of his way to save 5-cents on a gallon of gasoline will, without flinching, pay $3.50 for a cup of Starbucks coffee, and $12 for a container of popcorn and a soft drink at a movie theater.

What makes this phenomenon "amazing" is that these people have to know, on some level—consciously or subconsciously—that for that same $12, they could go to a supermarket and buy a *case* of soft drinks and enough raw popcorn kernels to make, literally, twenty or thirty containers of theater popcorn.

And of course, as if the mark-up on movie beverages isn't already exorbitant (what's the wholesale cost of a squirt of syrup and some carbonated water?), these customers drive the profit margin even higher by uttering the three words every concessionaire longs to hear: "Extra ice, please." Yep, fill that canister so full of ice, it will barely require any "cost" ingredients at all.

There are bars in Santa Monica that sell a bottle of imported beer for $9. That computes to $54 a six-pack. Mind you, we're not talking about paying top dollar for some exotic dish prepared in a specialty restaurant, something you could never hope to duplicate at home. We're talking about paying $54 for the identical six-pack you can buy at your local liquor store for a fraction of the price.

When I bring up these grim economic facts to friends (yes, even on my "consumer" high-horse, I've managed to keep a few friends), they pooh-pooh me; they argue that my examples are bogus comparisons, that you can't look at it that way, that what you're really paying for is "service." Some of them have even said, cryptically, that it "all evens out in the end," whatever that means.

But there's a larger issue here. Not to sound holier-than-thou, but it should be noted that the same people who willingly pay $14 for a hot dog and cup of beer at Dodger Stadium—who impulsively blow $15.99 for Season One of "Hill Street Blues" (and then never get around to watching it)—are resistant to giving immigrant workers a leg up.

It's hard to explain. When it comes to sharing our purse with those who toil at society's crappiest jobs, we become less generous. For whatever reason, when given the opportunity to spread it around to those on the bottom, we tend to hold out.

The same people who tip Las Vegas casino dealers don't leave a nickel for the housekeepers who clean their hotel rooms. The same patrons who are willing to pay $18 (say what??) for a deluxe mango margarita at an upscale LA restaurant—and then leave a commensurate gratuity for the actress-cum-waitress—don't bother tipping the guys at the local carwash who work their tails off.

One could almost applaud this willingness to throw away money on wildly frivolous stuff—write it off as some post-millennial, "easy-come, easy-go" mentality—if only these good people would throw their money at manual laborers the same way they throw it at blackjack dealers and cocktail waitresses. But they don't.

Instead, they argue with Mexican gardeners over their rates, and complain about how lazy their Mexican baby-sitters are. They haggle with those day-laborers outside Home Depot, trying to convince them to clear their whole goddamn backyard for $50. They won't slip the trash collector so much as $10 at Christmas.

People are already complaining about the increase in the minimum wage. The same people who have no problem with monthly cable TV fees rising every month for no apparent reason, regard an increase in the minimum wage as unfair.

A person I know (an insurance executive) fears the increase could actually destabilize the economy by (drum roll, please) "causing inflation." He's the same guy who supports a trillion-dollar banking bailout, the same guy who opposes limiting executive compensation. Alas, he's the same guy who orders "extra ice."

CounterPunch
2009

WHAT A DEMOCRATIC REGIME CAN DO FOR LABOR

Even with the "damage" that was supposedly done by Clinton's taunts, innuendo and ideological body blows during the Obama vs. Clinton primary (e.g., Obama's inexperience and naivete, the Reverend Wright connection, his inferior health care plans, etc.), the residue of a botched war, a failing economy, and eight years of criminal levels of deception and cronyism will be enough to propel Obama into the White House.

Despite having a highly motivated attack dog in Sarah Palin, out there looking to smear her opponents and distort the record, that towering mountain of post-Bush bad news and bad memories will simply prove too large for John McCain to dig out from under.

So how will having a Democrat in the White House, for the first time in eight years, benefit organized labor?

Nostalgia addicts, ex-Wobblies, socialists, Ramsey Clark progressives, and other labor "radicals" will doubtless caution union members not to hold their breath. They'll say that the Democrats bring nothing to the picnic other than empty rhetoric, that they're little more than Establishment shills who are part of the same useless, corrupt system as the Republicans.

But that view is not only cynical, it's unhelpful; more than that, it's downright self-defeating. Yes, the Democrats have much to answer for. Yes, they have let the unions down. There's no denying that. Despite organized labor's years of party loyalty, not to mention tens of millions of dollars in donations, the Democrats have disgraced themselves by running for cover whenever the going got tough, fearful of being identified as unequivocally "pro-union," and for that they deserve labor's contempt.

But the relationship has also been demonstrably (and confoundingly) contradictory. While the Democrats have been labor's most frustrating disappointment, they also, like it or not, have been labor's sole benefactor.

Labor needs to face a stark and frightening reality: Until things change (and that could be a while . . . like *forever*), we're all going to continue swimming in the same tank. And that tank happens to be the two-party system. Putting our cynicism aside, we need to recognize that there are several pro-labor moves the newly elected Barack Obama can be expected to make, and three moves—*three moves*—he's guaranteed to make immediately.

The first will be to install a new Secretary of Labor; and with that new Secretary comes a whole cabinet-level group of labor activists. The second will be to begin appointing fresh members to the 5-member NLRB (National Labor Relations Board). Both of these moves will not only have enormous significance for labor, but they're ones that can be pulled off with little or no resistance.

The way the NLRB is set up, the president controls three of its five seats, and the opposition party controls the other two. The 5-year terms of service are staggered, with one member leaving and another being appointed each year. The General Counsel to the NLRB serves a 4-year term, corresponding to that of U.S. president. Obama will stack the Board with like-minded Democrats, replacing the Bush-appointed, anti-labor minions who are currently serving and who have consistently ruled against labor during two consecutive Republican administrations.

It's the NLRB who oversees union organizing and elections in this country, and who, if vigilant and committed, can be an important ally to labor. A proactive, pro-labor NLRB can be counted upon to ride roughshod over the landscape, prosecuting employers who violate federal labor law by using coercion, intimidation or threats to prevent employees from joining a union. Wal-Mart immediately comes to mind. A new Board would be anathema to the giant retailer. It's a start.

The third move is a huge one: With Obama leading the charge, the Democrats will push to get the EFCA (Employee Free Choice Act) passed. Under the EFCA, employees would be permitted to join a union without having to go through the hassle of sanctioning an NLRB election; all they'd be required to do is sign cards indicating that they wish to join (known as the "card check" method). If a majority signs such cards, the NLRB would be authorized to recognize the union as the employees' exclusive representative in the collective bargaining process. Simple as that.

Another key feature of the EFCA is that it requires labor and management to submit to an arbitration board in the event that they were unable to agree on a "first" contract. The parties would be given 120 days to reach a settlement. If unable to agree to a contract during that period, the arbitration board would have full power to settle the dispute. That's a staggering amount of authority to give a third party.

In March of 2007, by a vote of 241 to 185, the House of Representatives passed the EFCA, but because a subsequent vote for cloture (which would have limited debate and moved the measure quickly to a vote) failed in the Senate, the bill got shelved. In any event, Bush had already promised to veto it. Getting the EFCA passed needed a Democratic president as the first step; with that done, it will need a minimum of 60 Democrats in the Senate, which, admittedly, will be a battle.

But it's already been hinted at that, as a possible compromise, the Democrats would be willing to withdraw the controversial arbitration board provision in return for Republican support. This is a critically important bill. Even without the arbitration provision, having a law on the books that gives the American worker automatic card check privileges would be a huge victory for organized labor.

There's lots of work ahead, and much of it—most of it—will be tedious. But instead of dwelling on what the Democrats aren't, labor advocates need to focus on what they are, on what they're willing to do to help. This isn't make-believe. We don't have the luxury of treating labor relations as some abstract exercise in social-economic theory. It's the real world. And in the real world tangible improvements tend to come in tiny, hard-fought increments.

As much as organized labor would love to see Taft-Hartley repealed, NAFTA overhauled or dismantled, and those obnoxious right-to-work states turn union, such things aren't likely to happen—at least not in the foreseeable future. Instead of harboring pipe dreams, labor radicals need to focus on what's obtainable. They need to throw in with the one group that has a realistic chance of getting something done: Obama and the Democrats.

Liberalati
2008

THE TWO-TIER WAGE FORMAT: CREATING CHAOS

People are stunned and confused when they learn that big-time unions such as the United Auto Workers (UAW) have agreed to contracts that contain two-tier wage provisions. It was organized labor (and not the Church or the U.S. Congress or philanthropic organizations) who first demanded equal pay and equal seniority for women. Equal pay for equal work was one of labor's fundamental tenets. So, to the casual observer, the notion of a union agreeing to something so unjust is inconceivable.

For those unfamiliar with the concept, a two-tier format requires new employees to earn less money than their senior co-workers. Even when doing identical jobs, even when working side by side. Because these tiered plans generally have no "sunset language" (built-in expiration dates), no amnesty periods, no mechanisms for equalizing pay, the rate discrepancies remain permanent.

Through natural attrition a company can eventually end up with its entire workforce earning substantially lower wages. Worse, the two-tier format doesn't apply exclusively to wages; it can cut into the entire economic package, including benefits. Newbies are commonly locked into lower vacation time, higher medical premiums and smaller pensions. That's why the tiered format is so tempting to businesses.

While the configuration has been around in one form or another for decades, it wasn't until the 1990s that it became a routine agenda item, and it wasn't until fairly recently that companies began treating it as a "deal-breaker." Arguably, the genie was let out of the bottle when companies first began adopting hiring rates (where new-hires aren't paid the full rate until they've been there a year), and when lump-sum bonuses were accepted in lieu of GWIs (General Wage Increases).

To a company looking to cut costs, paying cash instead of a GWI is a sophisticated short cut to achieving it. Because overtime is computed at the (old) hourly rate, as are vacation and holiday pay, sick leave, workers comp claims, and pension formulas, the overall savings to a company can be considerable.

But even with these precursors in play, how was organized labor ever persuaded to accept a provision so toxic and self-destructive as this?

Typically, management comes at the union from two angles, one economic, one cultural. The economic approach bluntly warns that without the adoption of a two-tier format, cost savings will be sought elsewhere. In this context, "elsewhere" is understood to mean benefits and wages, two components of the membership's Holy Trinity (the third is seniority). And the benefit considered most vulnerable is health care.

Since the early 1990s, the threat of unleashing the hounds of medical insurance has been management's most effective scare tactic. Because everyone who follows the news knows that medical costs are out of control and spiraling upward, the fear of a family budget being wiped out by exorbitant premiums and deductibles looms large.

The company begins by bombarding the union with reams of grim statistics: comparisons to other facilities, other industries, other unions, other states, other countries, other eras. In a normal contract negotiation, while economics (particularly wages) are always foremost and omnipresent, they manage somehow to stay muted and unobtrusive, like background music, until crunch time. But in a two-tier wage pitch the demands are unrelenting and merciless, right from the get-go.

The company recites the names of businesses that have already moved to Mississippi or Malaysia, or have shut down altogether because they couldn't compete. They mention the hundreds of thousands of layoffs in the sector; they compare GM's national strike in 1970, where over 400,000 workers walked off their jobs to GM's recent strike, where 73,000 walked out; they note that during their last hiring period, nearly 2,000 people showed up to apply for 44 hourly positions; and they mention that virtually no one in the facility ever quits to seek employment elsewhere, because they're all so well-paid.

It's an assault, an avalanche of bad news. The union is told, analogously, that it can choose to swallow a bitter pill (and maybe choke on it a bit) or it can choose to undergo major surgery. The choice is yours. Do you want your medical plan to remain intact, or do you want your premiums to skyrocket? By giving the company the relief it seeks in the area of future wages, you can hang on to what you have. The choice is yours. That's the economic argument.

The cultural argument is subtler and more tantalizing. Not only is the union reminded that the plan won't adversely affect anyone currently on the payroll, these future new-hires, these people who are going to be making less money than the rest of them, are portrayed as being vaguely *culpable*, as if their Johnny-come-lately status makes them somehow deserving of being punished.

Current employees—those who've faithfully put in their years and showed their loyalty to both union and company—will continue to be rewarded for that service. Besides being grandfathered in, and having their precious medical insurance untouched, the company will offer them a hefty "signing bonus" for ratifying the contract.

Because this enterprise can be seen as class warfare once removed (a case of the working class arranging things so as to form its own sub-class), management reassures the union that the only people who can be "hurt" by this are people who do not yet exist. They are "hypothetical" workers, part of that sea of nameless, faceless job applicants who may one day seek employment in the facility.

Moreover, when these folks move from hypothetical to "actual," they are going to know exactly what's in store for them. The two-tier format will be carefully explained.   If the prospect of earning as much as $16 per hour on the bottom tier (as opposed to $30 per hour on the top tier) makes economic sense to them, they'll be welcomed aboard.

But if the deal offends them (if the notion of equal work being rewarded with *unequal* pay is something they simply can't abide), they'll be congratulated for having a well-developed sense of justice, and cautioned not to let the door hit them on the way out.

And that, more or less, is how the two-tier plan is pitched.

Of course, once these plans are implemented, they're an ungodly mess. The membership experiences an agonizing case of "buyer's remorse." The same members who assumed they could work comfortably with sacrificial lambs now feel pangs of conscience. They blame the company; they blame themselves; they blame the union for bringing it to a vote. And then there's that whole dynamic of the haves bickering with the have-nots; morale plummets, and union solidarity goes out the window.

But as bad as it gets, it's nothing compared to later. The *really* bad news doesn't come until the next negotiation, after the two-tier format is firmly in place. That's when the company announces that, unfortunately, medical insurance, the one benefit that was to be left untouched, must now be drastically slashed. And when the union screams bloody murder, they're told it's business. Just business.

CounterPunch
2007

ARE LABOR UNIONS READY FOR PRIME TIME?

Despite the AFL-CIO's prodigious efforts to attract new members—not to mention the existence of 35-40 million "working poor," desperately in need of livable wages, pensions and medical coverage—union membership continues to slip. What was once a robust 35 percent (during the 1950s) is now hovering at a fraction more than a precarious 12 percent.

It's been reported that the AFL-CIO has spent, literally, hundreds of millions of dollars on its organizing efforts. That's a lot of money, with precious little to show for it. The recent Wal-Mart organizing drive stands as a perfect example of labor's grim struggle to increase its membership.

With more than 3,600 Wal-Mart stores in the U.S. to choose from, and despite bringing to bear all the financial and strategic resources at its disposal, the mighty House of Labor couldn't persuade a single one of the giant retailer's stores to join the union. Not one store. That's not just disappointing, that's scary.

While the AFL-CIO has to assume responsibility for the Wal-Mart debacle, nobody is really "blaming" them. Ask anyone who's ever done it, and they'll tell you that recruiting new members is the toughest, bleakest, most thankless union job there is. But labor's woeful track record may be evidence that a new approach is needed, something to reinvigorate the organizing effort.

Perhaps it's time for labor to change its basic philosophy of organizing, and abandon that tired, old Holy Trinity: i.e., rallies, townhall meetings, and hand-billing prospective members. Maybe it's time to adopt a Madison Avenue marketing approach.

If unions are willing to spend their money—tons of it—on organizing drives, then let them spend it on something that has half a chance of succeeding. Let the unions seek to reinvent themselves by appealing to a far larger and more diverse audience. Let them take their act to prime-time television.

The persuasive power of TV advertising can't be disputed. Although no one *honestly* believes that a wealthy young athlete would choose a Buick sedan over, say, a sleek Mercedes-Benz or flashy Corvette, General Motors nonetheless managed to sell thousands of Buicks simply by showing a smiling Tiger Woods sitting behind the wheel of a LaCrosse CX. The Buick commercial was, by all accounts, wildly successful. Madison Avenue may be soulless, but it isn't wrong: Image is everything.

Yes, TV commercials are pricey, and yes, it's a bit unorthodox (if not undignified) to be schlepping something as socially "noble" as labor unions in-between those beer and cell phone ads. Still, if television advertising proves more effective than the traditional, eat-your-spinach approach that labor has been flogging for over a century, orthodoxy won't matter.

Organized labor needs an image transplant. It needs to launch a celebrity spokesman of its own, someone hip and charismatic, someone who transcends all that stodgy proletarianism. If Tiger Woods can convince people to buy his grandpa's car, why can't a celebrity athlete or entertainer convince working people to consider joining a union?

Granted, going out and buying a new car isn't the same thing as joining a workers' collective. But having a celebrity look into a TV camera and testify to how important unions have been, historically, and how valuable they can still be to workers seeking to improve their economic lives, is going to get people's attention. A pitch like that, played repetitiously, could make a difference.

Moreover, if Hollywood is even half as "liberal" as it's supposed to be, there should be no shortage of entertainers willing to step up to the plate. After all, isn't every working actor a dues-paying member of SAG (Screen Actors Guild)? And if common ideology isn't inducement enough to attract a spokesman, then let the money talk. Make it too lucrative to turn down.

Of course, choosing the right celebrity will be crucial. Because their political agendas are high-profile and polarizing, Sean

Penn, Alec Baldwin, Tim Robbins, the Dixie Chicks, et al, need not apply. Image is everything. A Vin Diesel urging Gen X'ers to join a union is one thing; a Johnny Depp doing it from a bistro in Paris, France, is another.

An inspired choice for this project would be rap artist Eminem. Where the AFL-CIO's earnest but anachronistic campaign couldn't convince Wal-Mart employees to sign union cards, an ultra-cool "Slim Shady," with his working-class roots and defiant, anti-establishment persona, might just pull it off. Eminem's fan base consists of young white males. How many of them work at Wal-Mart?

An obvious question: Would Eminem agree to do it? Would this anti-establishment icon be willing to make a commercial? Put it this way: Would he accept a few million dollars to tape a 30-second spot that simultaneously inspires blue-collar workers to improve their economic lives, rubs Corporate America's nose in the dirt, and benefits the United Auto Workers, whose headquarters happen to be in his hometown of Detroit?

Dude, what's not to like?

CounterPunch
2008

A UNION STORY

Some years ago, the Kimberly-Clark Corporation hired an employee (I'll call him "Lee") into its paper mill in Fullerton, California. A large, modern facility, the Fullerton mill manufactured tons of raw paper each shift and produced, among other things, Kleenex facial tissue and Huggies disposal diapers. It employed 700 hourly workers, all of whom belonged to the AWPPW (Association of Western Pulp and Paper Workers).

Lee was a man in his early thirties, married, with two young kids, who'd been out of work for several months. He told everyone that the wages and benefits K-C offered were a godsend. Lee's wife had previously worked in an office but had slipped on the tile floor in the company's bathroom and hurt her back so severely that she couldn't continue working, and was in the process of taking her employer to court in a Workers Compensation dispute.

In those days, the training of new-hires was done by an hourly employee, usually a person in the same job classification, usually the person with the most seniority on that job. Typically, training took two or three weeks. At the completion of training the employee was placed on the progression ladder and scheduled for the shift and crew his seniority dictated, earning the same rate of pay as anyone else doing that particular job on that particular shift.

There was no extra compensation for length of service or experience. You were either qualified or unqualified for a job, with no gradations or in-between status. "Equal pay for equal work" was the union mantra. No games were played, no one received extra money for being "more qualified," no one jumped the seniority ladder or got a cushier job because he was buddies with the shift supervisor.

Union seniority guaranteed that no matter what your age, gender or ethnicity, once you were deemed qualified, you were scheduled where your seniority put you and you received the pay of the job you worked. Just one of the many virtues of union membership.

The probationary period for new employees was 60 days. That meant that during your first two months on the job, you could be fired at will, instantly, for any reason (or no reason), without appeal and without access to union representation. After 60 days it was a different story. After 60 days you were a full-fledged union member, entitled to the same representation as any other member in good standing.

Lee's problem wasn't obvious to everyone, at least not at first. There was no question he could do the job; he could do it better than average when he felt like it. The problem was, the only time he seemed to feel like it was when he was trying to impress someone or when a supervisor happened to be in the area. On those occasions he performed heroically. However, on other occasions, which was most of the time, he was looking for ways to get out of work or just going through the motions, pretending to appear busy.

Not everyone who walks through the front door of a manufacturing plant is production worker material. The place operates 24-hours a day. The job can be demanding. While the union pay and benefits are decent, and the overtime plentiful, the work can be arduous or monotonous, the hours are crazy (nights and graveyard, back-end and front-end 12-hour shifts, double-shifts), and advancement comes via seniority rather than "merit." It's not for everyone.

The person who trained Lee (we'll call her "Mary") was a woman who'd worked in the mill for 12 years. She'd once served as an elected department shop steward and was respected by her crew. With Lee only a week or two short of finishing his 60-day trial, Mary approached a union rep, the vice-president of Local 672, and told him that, in her opinion and in the opinion of people on the floor, Lee shouldn't be allowed to complete his probation. He should be let go immediately.

The union rep could see that "betraying" a fellow employee gave Mary no pleasure. In fact, it was obvious she was very uncomfortable being the bearer of such treacherous news and had struggled with her decision. But she felt compelled to do it for the good of the department.

Mary told the rep that not only was Lee a goof-off and opportunist, he'd been asking everyone about K-C's medical leave and Workers Comp policies, sniffing around for information on how one collected money on a job-related injury (e.g., asking how long people typically stayed out on medicals, asking if they had a "light duty" policy for injured employees, etc.). The view on the floor was that if Lee were to be hired permanently, he'd be a lousy partner, an unreliable relief, and a chronic system abuser.

Of course, the obvious question was: What had K-C management been doing all this time? What were the bosses looking for during this Lee's probationary period? How closely were they monitoring him? How concerned were they by what they'd observed?

The answer is that management had paid virtually no attention to Lee. Because he hadn't caused any obvious trouble and had maintained acceptable attendance, as far as they were concerned the guy was good to go. While one would think the company would place an enormous premium on insuring that only "quality" workers were hired in, that wasn't the case.

But it did matter to the union. Because the last thing Local 672 needed was another bad apple in the barrel, the vice-president took it upon himself to get this problem fixed. After all, the union's reputation and continued prosperity depended upon its members performing efficiently, earning their keep. The Kimberly-Clark mill was a for-profit enterprise, competing in the open market. No one wanted another game-player or deadbeat added to the crew . . . *no one*, not even the other deadbeats already on the payroll.

The rep met privately with a department supervisor and relayed exactly what Mary had reported. He told him everything, making certain not to leave out any of the alarming details.

What happened next was unfortunate but, given the company's history, no big surprise.

The supervisor thanked him for coming forward and promised to take the "necessary steps." And that was the end of it. Nothing more was done. Two weeks later, Lee cleared probation and became a union member in good standing. The crews were disappointed. Once again, management had not only disregarded the union's sincerity and expertise, but had, in fact, resented what they saw as union poaching on company turf. It was management arrogance and laziness, plain and simple, that kept Lee from being cut loose.

All of which brings us to California's public school teachers. For the last several years Governor Arnold Schwarzeneggar, along with Republican members of the state assembly and the state's school administrators, have been trying to blame the teachers' union for California's low test scores.

Rather than identifying such factors as a dramatic shift in the state's demographics, or a drop in per capita funds for education, or chronic absenteeism, or language handicaps, or the breakdown of the American family, or the "politicization" of the curriculum, etc., they tried to pin the blame on the same union teachers who, for decades, had contributed to California being routinely regarded as one of the best school systems in the country.

Think about that. When California was regularly ranked in the top two or three states in the country, these very same union teachers were running the classrooms, getting sterling results, winning awards, and, in the eyes of the administrators, doing everything right. But now, with the public schools plagued by a staggering array of problems, it's suddenly the union's fault. The bosses are pretending that California's teachers are no longer competent to teach.

Arguably, not everyone who walks through the front door of a school is cut out for teaching, despite having a valid teaching credential. Under the current contract, new teachers remain on probation for 2 years. And during that time they can be fired

162

without cause, for any reason, and without recourse to union representation or the grievance procedure.

During the last contract negotiations with the LAUSD (Los Angeles Unified School District) Schwarzeneggar and company attempted to get the probation period extended to 5 years. The union successfully resisted, arguing that, if management did the job they were supposed to do, 2 years was more than long enough.

While a sub-standard worker can, conceivably, fool his bosses for 60 days, no one—school teacher, production worker, medical doctor or policeman—can pass himself off as a good employee for *2 full years*, not if the bosses are halfway diligent in their scrutiny. It can't be done. Two years is simply too long to "fake" it.

The Kimberly-Clark and LAUSD instances are two examples of the same management defect: a reluctance to make difficult personnel decisions, coupled with a willingness to blame a convenient third party—in this case, a labor union. The level of gutlessness and self-satisfaction displayed in this version of "management" is startling. That it is endemic to the business community makes it no less pathetic.

As for Lee, he worked at the mill for several years before surprising everyone by abruptly quitting after getting divorced. He remained a marginal worker the whole time he was there. He goofed off, ducked out of tough assignments, began missing work, and took questionable medical leaves. Mary's initial assessment couldn't have been more accurate.

Instead of moving against him (reprimanding him, hounding him, instilling him with the fear of God), K-C management preferred to overlook his shortcomings. They either ignored him or, when on the war path, threw up their hands in despair and blamed the union contract for "protecting" him.

As for Lee's fellow employees, they had no choice. Because the jobs needed to get done despite having a marginal worker on the crew, they did what good people regularly do in any work setting, union or non-union.

Without an additional nickel in compensation or so much as a word of gratitude from the company, they picked up the slack. They carried him the whole time.

CounterPunch
2008

EXTRA, EXTRA! INDUSTRY CRUMBLING!

On Wednesday night (July 22), unionized employees of the Boston Globe—members of the Boston Newspaper Guild—voted 366 to 179 to accept massive wage and benefit cuts in order keep the venerable, 137-year old newspaper afloat.

This outcome followed an earlier vote, more than a month ago, where the membership narrowly (by a margin of 12 votes) turned down a similar contract offer. The difference between that vote and this one was, ostensibly, the result of some slight movement on the company's part and, alas, a crushing sense of dread on the part of the Guild's 700 members, which include editorial, advertising and clerical staff.

The concessions include significant pay cuts, forced furloughs and uncompensated vacation leave, elimination of job security provisions and severe slashing of the health and pension benefits. In short, it's an across-the-board reduction of the entire collective bargaining package, reminiscent of the succession of staggering cuts the UAW (United Auto Workers) has been forced to make ever since the mid-1990s.

Even with the massive concessions, the Globe (owned by the New York Times Company), is not out of the woods. According to Guild president Dan Totten, the Times Co. had announced going into negotiations that, at the very minimum, it needed a $20 million payroll reduction to avoid shutting down the paper.

Still, some skeptics have suggested that it's all part of an elaborate power-play to bust the union, that because the newspaper is on the market—with the Times Co. aggressively courting potential buyers—the company was looking to reduce its contractual liability to make the acquisition more attractive.

Ultimately, despite the suspicions, mutual recriminations, and dragging out of negotiations for more than three months, Guild members had little choice but ratifying the agreement. After all, what were their options? Vote it down and dare the Globe to go out of business? People need to work, and they'll do practically anything to avoid economic suicide.

To that point, it should be remembered that employees of the infamous Three Mile Island nuclear facility petitioned the government to allow them to return to work after the accident even though the plant was classified as radioactively "contaminated." Why would they risk returning to a dangerous facility? Because they needed the work.

Two phenomena continue to defy explanation. One is working people who gloat when they hear that union members (like the Guild or UAW) are forced to make concessions to management. The other is low or low-middle-class workers who stubbornly oppose raising the taxes of the very wealthy.

Arguably, given the eccentricities of human nature, you can *almost* understand the first phenomenon. You can write it off to petty jealously or resentment. You can put yourself in their place and more or less understand how non-union workers would experience a jolt of satisfaction at seeing their better compensated unionized brethren get "payback."

Still, it's a bizarre and lamentable mindset. Lemon-sucking right-wing Republicans wanting to see a union get hammered is bad enough, but underpaid, under-insured working people wanting to see it happen is not only disappointing, it's self-defeating.

The second phenomenon is more disturbing. Just as there is something refreshingly healthy and life-affirming about wanting the very rich to pay more taxes, there's something morbid and sick about *not* wanting it. For working people earning $40,000 annually it should be a natural reflex—a survival instinct—to want investment bankers earning $10 million to pay more taxes.

And we're not discussing economic theories here, with their attendant formulas, graphs, and charts. We're talking about one's fundamental outlook on the world. We're talking about the kind of egalitarianism that puts a fire in the belly of an underdog and causes him to rejoice when the extravagantly privileged are forced to acknowledge their shared humanity.

A poor man fighting on behalf of the wealthy—doing all he can to help the rich get richer—is not only irrational, it's self-destructive. It's like the fox going out and buying running shoes for the hounds.

Some years ago I had a conversation with "Fred" at the union hall. Fred was a shipping checker working in a warehouse, I was a union rep. We were friends. I knew his family. The subject of tax brackets arose, and I was stunned and annoyed when he declared, almost defiantly, that he was opposed to the wealthy paying more taxes.

Fred was an Army veteran, a patriot, a self-described "libertarian," and a diligent worker respected by his peers, whose dream was to start his own landscaping business. It gives me no pleasure to admit that, because I didn't have the patience to approach the issue by nibbling around its edges, I went straight for the jugular.

I told Fred that Wall Street loves fools like him. They love gullible, simple-minded poor people who work hard, pay their taxes, and, yet, oppose forcing these parasitic Wall Street bastards to part with their money. "They view you as the perfect stooge," I told him. "A poor man fighting for the interests of the rich."

Granted, what I said was self-righteous and overheated, but it got the point across. However, Fred's answer still confounds and haunts me. He calmly said, "I plan to have my own business someday, and I don't want the government taking my money."

The Exception Magazine
2009

RALPH'S MANAGEMENT INDICTED

Although the announcement didn't get much play in the media, on Friday, September 19, a federal grand jury handed down indictments against eight former and current Ralphs management employees, accusing them of 23 counts of violating federal labor law. The alleged violations occurred five years ago, during the UCFW's (United Commercial and Food Workers) debilitating 141-day strike against Ralphs grocery store chain.

Two years ago, store executives pleaded guilty to similar charges (and paid fines amounting to $20 million), admitting that during the company's lockout they had knowingly and illegally hired hundreds of union workers to help keep the stores running smoothly. Friday's indictments were a follow-up to those original charges.

The case was ugly from the outset. Once the UCFW called its strike (in October, 2003), Ralphs locked out employees at all of their stores. However, it soon became apparent that the grocery operation was suffering from not having enough competent, experienced workers to run it. As tantalizing as the notion was, hiring back selected locked-out employees to man up the stores was illegal, and Ralphs knew it.

Still, because the strike/lockout was crippling them, Ralphs managers came up with a plan that, simultaneously, addressed their manpower needs and concealed their crime. They tried a con game. They assigned these illegal hires fictitious names and phony social security numbers, and scheduled them to work at stores a good distance away from their usual jobs, so they wouldn't be recognized by fellow workers or regular customers. Unfortunately for Ralphs, the subterfuge was almost immediately exposed.

Of course, when accusations of misconduct were initially made by the UCFW, Ralphs not only categorically denied them, they pretended to be grossly offended by even the hint that such improprieties had occurred, going so far as to describe the charges as proof that the union was "vindictive" and "desperate."

Only after an overwhelming amount of evidence had been amassed against them did company executives sheepishly acknowledge their crimes. In addition to the $20 million paid in fines, Ralphs agreed to establish a $50 million fund to reimburse union members for money lost by Ralphs having extended the duration of the shutdown (by keeping stores running via illegal employees).

In any event, most observers thought the stiff fines and the employee reimbursement fund would be the end of it. But because the violations were so crass, so clumsy and heavy-handed—and because Ralphs executives had lied so shamelessly throughout the investigation—the U.S. attorneys decided that the grocery chain executives needed to be treated as the criminals they were. The feds deserve credit for persevering.

Strikes have been part of the labor-management landscape for over 200 years. The historical rationale behind striking is a simple one. In order to put pressure on a company to be more generous in its contract offer, the union attempts to demonstrate to management just how much the company needs their workers, how dependent upon them they are.

And the only way for workers to do this is by withholding their labor—to "punish" themselves by voluntarily sacrificing their immediate wages, benefits and job security in return for a greater, long-term good. The logic underlying a strike can be expressed by the simple dictum: By hurting ourselves, we can, perhaps, hurt you.

In truth, a strike is the only *real* leverage a union has. Short of actually shutting down a company, everything else in a contract negotiation amounts to rhetoric—debating, bickering, compromising, shouting, threatening. Moreover, despite what management says about strikes being obsolete, meaningless, counterproductive, etc., don't let them kid you. Strikes are the only weapon management fears.

So when a company like Ralphs secretly and illegally hires hundreds of locked-out workers and continues to run its operations, it's sending a phony message. It's saying that it doesn't miss the striking workers, that the operation is chugging along quite nicely without them, that the strike was unsuccessful.

Worse, Ralphs' felonies contributed to prolonging the strike, resulting not only in thousands of earnest strikers remaining out of work longer than necessary—unaware that laws were being broken—but forcing the union to accept significant contract concessions as a condition for returning to work

The Ralphs debacle should be a lesson to anyone who thinks Corporate America is predisposed to act ethically when it comes to labor relations. Alas, more often than not, the governing consideration in these matters—especially when the stakes are high—is whether or not they're likely to get caught. Thanks to the feds' persistence (and Ralphs own arrogance and stupidity), they *got* caught.

CounterPunch
2008

LABOR NEEDS A SOUTHERN STRATEGY

In case you haven't noticed, most of the really good manufacturing jobs still left in the U.S. are being moved to the Deep South. It's like a vast animal migration. Think of caribou. And why *wouldn't* companies want to move there? Cheap labor, no unions, lax pollution standards, huge tax incentives, lucrative subsidies, and the absence of urban blight. Hell, it's a corporation's dream.

With every major foreign automaker—Mercedes, BMW, Toyota, Honda, Kia, Nissan, Hyundai, Volvo—already having billion-dollar assembly plants in states like Alabama, Tennessee, and Georgia, in another twenty years or so, Dixie will be what Detroit was in its heyday.

And with Dixie as the New Detroit, what will the Old Detroit be? It will be what it is today, only more so: a sprawling urban wasteland, part of the ever-growing Rust Belt. In twenty years, American college students will speak of the economic vitality of 1960s Detroit the way they speak of the grandeur of Ancient Rome and Athens.

Labor's only hope is to organize the South. They need to do whatever it takes to recruit new union members. Sponsor rodeos. Sponsor gun shows. Sponsor chili cook-offs, monster truck pulls, pee-wee sports leagues. Hire Tennessee Titan and Atlanta Falcon football players to do radio and TV spots. Start your own record company, produce country music using home-grown musicians, and put a union-made American flag on your label.

To gain a foothold, organized labor needs to embark upon the Mother of All Public Relations Campaigns. It should consider putting together a racing team and entering a car in a NASCAR event. The Teamsters and the SEIU should jointly sponsor a "Change to Win" racing team, using local drivers. What labor needs more than anything is positive exposure, and lots of it.

Unions should begin making conspicuous donations to impoverished high school football teams in the region, offering to buy new uniforms. The IAM should make a big deal of inaugurating scholarship programs. The Steelworkers should give $5,000 grants to deserving high school students, naming him or her as their annual "Student of Steel."

The AFT (American Federation of Teachers) should establish a generous endowment at the University of Alabama, tied in, perhaps, to the formation of a Chair in Labor Relations. The AFL-CIO should announce that it's going to donate money for a new athletic facility at LSU. The IBEW (International Brotherhood of Electrical Workers) should set up vocational apprenticeship programs at community colleges.

Fortunately, one thing Big Labor still has plenty of—at least for now—is money; but it needs to spend that money more wisely. Big Labor needs to take the cure—it needs to quit depending on sympathetic, smooth-talking Democrats to carry its water. Clearly, the American South is where their resources should be focused.

Some smart guy (it may have been labor historian Irving Bernstein, in *The Lean Years*) once suggested that big-time labor unions should move their national headquarters from Washington D.C. and relocate to a large southern city, like Atlanta, Georgia or Nashville, Tennessee. It's a brilliant idea.

If you got ten or twelve of America's largest unions to relocate to the metropolitan South, and offer its employees top wages and benefits for routine clerical work, word would spread. Working for a national labor union would now be coveted position. ("Hey, where do you work?" "I work for the Teamsters.").

By becoming an integral part of a municipal economy in the Deep South, organized labor will have effectively infiltrated enemy lines without, figuratively, firing a shot (i.e., without anyone even having to join a union). Brilliant.

The only reason most blue-chip unions in America (the UAW is a notable exception, with its headquarters at Solidarity House, in Detroit) have their offices in D.C. is, ostensibly, to mingle with the nation's power brokers. More accurately, it's a convenient way for slick lobbyists and predatory Democratic politicians to take the AFL-CIO's money.

But hasn't that relationship been one sorry, monumental scam? I mean, what tangible benefits have been gained by being at the epicenter of America's political power? In the 62 years since the Taft-Hartley Act—arguably the most anti-union legislation in U.S. history—organized Labor has poured tens of millions of dollars into efforts to get the Act repealed or, at the minimum, significantly modified, and virtually nothing has come of it.

Instead, organized labor continues to be marginalized, national membership rolls continue to be chipped away, and union members across the country continue to be demoralized.

So why stay in Washington? Why not move to Dixie, where the battles of the next several decades will almost certainly be fought? At the very least, the commercial real estate will be much cheaper.

ON BEING TRAMPLED TO DEATH AT WAL-MART

Not to be morbid, but if we all had to choose a way to die, most of us probably wouldn't pick something as gruesome as being trampled to death by frenzied bargain-hunters at a neighborhood discount store.

And not to be morally condescending, but if we had to choose the worst possible image of American consumers—a snapshot depicting us as the mindless, de-humanized, materialistic fiends much of the world thinks we are—the November 28 Wal-Mart stampede in New York, which resulted in the death of a store employee, would be it.

Indeed, one could argue that the Wal-Mart death is to fanatical consumerism what Abu Ghraib was to America's military occupation of Iraq. It's hard to conceive of a more vivid or devastating image.

That it occurred on the doorstep of the earth's largest retailer of Third World merchandise, and the most celebrated and defiantly anti-union corporation in the world—and that the employee who was killed was one Jdi Mytai Damour, a 34-year old Haitian national—adds a weird, Orwellian quality to this tragic, mind-boggling episode.

No, we're not suggesting that this incident could *only* have occurred at Wal-Mart, or, for that matter, only at a non-union facility. Accidents can happen anywhere. We all know that. There have been fatal stampedes at European soccer games, Asian religious pilgrimages and American rock concerts, so this is not something we're trying to pin exclusively on a big-time merchandiser, union or non-union.

But let's be honest. Wal-Mart has a well-deserved reputation for not only doing "more with less," but for ruthlessly driving down costs, employing the fewest possible workers, and utilizing bare-bone "skeleton" crews. And it did expect a huge crowd on this occasion. Therefore, it shouldn't be out of bounds to ask whether they were looking to save a buck or two.

It shouldn't be out of bounds to ask whether Wal-Mart had willfully scrimped on the number of security people they hired for Black Friday—despite the fact that this was going to be, unquestionably, the busiest shopping day of the year—or whether the security people they had in place had been adequately trained. It's a fair question.

Again, no one is saying the incident was wholly Wal-Mart's fault. There's no denying that these eager shoppers were a restless and unruly group. Indeed, local police had been called in earlier to calm down the antsy crowd, many of whom had been gathered there since before midnight, awaiting the store's 5:00 a.m. opening.

Still, because it was Wal-Mart's own security staff (and not the local cops) who was responsible for crowd control, we need to be reminded that quality, unfortunately, costs money. Attracting quality employees costs money, and providing employees with quality training costs money. Wal-Mart may live off the slogan, "Everyday low prices," but there's another slogan, a time-honored bromide, that comes into play as well: "You get what you pay for."

Also, upon closer inspection, those aforementioned examples of stampedes don't quite apply here. When you have tens of thousands of people at a rock concert or sports event, and they suddenly, inexplicably surge forward, the spectators in front, those pinned against barricades, are likely to be crushed. Macabre as it is, the simple "physics" involved explains what can happen.

But this Wal-Mart stampede was different. By all accounts, this was no sudden, spontaneous crowd swell, energized by the sheer inertia of tens of thousands of people inching forward. This was a crowd of a 2,000 anxious people looking to be the first ones at the bargain rack.

And this crowd didn't crush *each other*. They didn't inadvertently injure those in the front of the pack by pinning them against an immovable object. Rather, they broke down the front door and knocked to the floor one of the very staff people hired to maintain order. And then they trampled him to death. Because there were bargains to be had.

But if Wal-Mart isn't to blame, who is? If Wal-Mart management is correct in righteously contending that all they did was advertise a big, monstrous, blow-out sale, and that the unfortunate "riot" that ensued was in no way their fault, then who's to blame?

Is it the customers? Do we blame the mob? Even though no one in that frenzied crowd believed, in their wildest dreams, that something as tragic as this could happen, do we blame those dedicated bargain-hunters for reverting to such primitive behavior at the mere prospect of toys on sale?

Do we blame the mall for not supplying more private security? Do we blame the police for not hanging around to make sure things didn't get ugly? Or do we blame ourselves? Do we blame the American System—that high-octane consumer mentality that dominates the country, declaring, You Are What You Own?

Most likely, we'll blame no one. We'll simply write it off as one of those unfortunate, "shit happens" stories that piques our interest on the evening news before we forget about it and move on to the next economic juggernaut awaiting us . . . Christmas.

The Exception Magazine
2008

WHAT DOES A RADICAL UNION LOOK LIKE?

There's a tremendous variation among labor unions—not only among the industries with which they're affiliated, but among the working people comprising their memberships. There's the guy toiling in an iron foundry in Indiana, the guy running a paper machine in Everett, Washington, the nurse tending patients in a San Francisco convalescent hospital. And there's George Clooney, Julia Roberts, Derek Jeter, Alex Rodriquez, Kobe Bryant and Tom Brady.

What do these folks have in common? They are all dues-paying members of labor unions, organizations dedicated to improving the wages, benefits and working conditions of the American worker. The first three individuals mentioned earn roughly $50,000-$60,000 a year, with decent benefits. The others—the actors and athletes—earn millions.

In Clooney and Roberts' case, it should be obvious that they don't come close to representing the "average" SAG (Screen Actors Guild) member, the overwhelming majority of whom, unfortunately, can't make a living acting, and require supplemental jobs to pay their rent. According to union figures, something like 90% of SAG members earn less than $10,000 a year as actors.

That's not the case for professional athletes. A pro sports union stands as a lush oasis in labor's otherwise barren wasteland. Take the MLBPA (Major League Baseball Players Association) for example. Its contract with team owners requires that the *lowest-paid* player earns more than the president of the United States. Labor relations at this rarefied level break down, more or less, to disputes between the millionaires and the billionaires.

During a strike I was involved in some years ago, the federal mediator who'd been assigned to our negotiations shared an anecdote with us. He said that the AFL-CIO had recently sponsored a union solidarity conference in Arizona (a right-to-work state!), and invited one union rep from virtually every union in America, including the MLBPA.

He told us that the AFL-CIO had to chuckle when it received the response from the baseball union. The spokesman said that, while a player rep would be happy to attend the conference, he was going to expect "several thousand dollars" in *appearance* money. After all, these guys were celebrities. They got paid to show up at functions. Ah, union solidarity.

Which brings us to the Service Employees International Union, America's largest union (with 1.9 million members). Lately, the SEIU has been taking flak not only from its own membership but from the executive boards of dissident unions. Although part of that can be written off to the petty jealousies and schadenfreude that stalk a high-profile organization, another part of it is understandable.

In truth, the SEIU has made some questionable decisions recently; it's been accused of moving too quickly and carelessly, and, simultaneously, of being too cozy and accommodating with management. To make matters worse, the Service Union's leadership has been receiving glowing, positively *gushing* reviews from—of all places—America's business community. Talk about your kiss of death.

The major criticism of the SEIU and its Ivy League-educated president, Andrew Stern, is that in its aggressive (some say "dictatorial") efforts to expand membership it has chosen to make some deals that appear to favor management and disadvantage the workers.

For example, it has agreed to no-strike clauses as a condition for management's "neutrality" in organizing drives. This is where a company promises not to sabotage a union election in return for the SEIU's promise that, if certified, it won't go on strike for a minimum of 7 to 10 years.

Consorting with management and stripping union members of their right to strike even before signing their first contract is something that's going to drive hardcore labor aficionados up the wall. Meanwhile, Stern flies off to China on a corporate jet as a guest of Lee Scott, Wal-Mart's CEO. Andy Stern may be an effective administrator, but a Harry Bridges (the beloved "common man," former-president of the Longshoremen's union) he ain't.

Another gripe is Stern's devotion to New Age labor philosophy. Despite an avalanche of evidence to the contrary, Stern preaches the view that, for unions to be successful in the future, labor and management need to put aside their ideological differences and join together to form symbiotic partnerships. Moreover, he regards as "cynics" or "dinosaurs" those union folks who fail to share this vision.

While Stern's enthusiasm and personal magnetism have attracted disciples, there are lots of skeptics out there who recall what happened the first time a major union jungled-up with management. That was approximately 30 years ago, when Douglas Fraser, president of the UAW (United Auto Workers), was given a seat on Chrysler's Board of Directors. In the years that followed, contracts were ravaged, promises were broken, and several hundred thousand union members lost their jobs.

But saying that Andy Stern is *bad* for the labor movement is an unfair rap, one he doesn't deserve. No matter what his harshest critics think, it can't be easy being the president of a union these days, not with staggering across-the-board losses of jobs and a decline in overall membership staring you in the face. Your options are severely limited.

On the one hand, as president of an International, you're committed to increasing the number of union members, recognizing that the only way labor is going to climb back into the picture is through increased membership. And to do that, you can't expect to come marching in all defiant and militant, because those days are over, at least for now.

On the other hand, if the only way to increase your membership is by diluting union contracts so badly that the members have little to show for it, other than wearing their union pins and receiving monthly newsletters, what's the point really?

Which raises a question: What would the model of a "radical" labor union be today? Would it be a wildly "bottom-up" democracy, where the members run the whole show? Would it be one where the executive board whips the membership into an ideological froth with its anti-management rhetoric? Would it be one that adopted a take-no-prisoners stance in its relations with management, no matter how unproductive that was?

It could be argued that—New Age philosophy aside—Stern's pragmatic approach is, weirdly, as good a model as any. Perhaps, what passes for a "radical" union these days is one that has, by necessity, re-cast itself; one that hasn't abandoned its fundamental principles, but is now willing to make questionable compromises in order to get its foot in the door.

Maybe there's more to that deceptive tactic of taking what they give you—of gaining an initial, modest foothold and attempting to build on it—than meets the eye. It shouldn't be forgotten that patiently chipping away at the edifice was exactly how management succeeded in breaking down labor unions in the first place.

Fortunately, some unions still have the leverage and whiskers to go on strike when necessary, and it's important they don't back off, despite what those well-oiled seminar leaders say about labor and management being on the same "team."

But for those workers who don't have that leverage, for those who are hanging on by their fingernails or, indeed, still looking for a way inside, it's a different story. Being patient and biding its time may be the only practical way for organized labor to regain its influence.

There's a saying in poker: "You can't win the hand if you're not in it." And accepting significantly less than you want (or need) as a means of getting a company to sign its first union contract may be the right move. Preposterous as it seems, given today's fragile labor climate, maybe it's even a "radical" move.

CounterPunch
2008

SERF'S UP IN HOLLYWOOD

Tinsel Town is addicted to "star power." As evidence, look no further than SAG's (Screen Actors Guild) latest contract with the AMPTP (Alliance of Motion Picture and Television Producers), and you'll see that, while the Alliance is willing to pay A-listers top dollar, they continue to chip away at the incomes of those "marginal" actors who live off residuals and supporting roles.

Your Alec Baldwins, Angelina Jolies and George Clooneys may not have to worry about what their cut of DVD sales will be, but thousands of lesser known (and, arguably, equally talented) SAG members do. Clearly, there are two classes of Hollywood actors: monarchs and serfs. Okay, *three*: monarchs, noblemen, and serfs.

A question: What do the animated classics, "Snow White and the Seven Dwarves," "Lady and the Tramp," "Cinderella," "Peter Pan," and "Bambi" all have in common? Answer: The voices were done by little known (often uncredited) actors, and not the big-name stars who regularly do voices today.

While these were all wildly successful cartoons (still making money, incidentally) it's fair to say that had the same Disney executives been around *then* that are around *today*, Tramp would've been voiced by Gary Cooper, and Snow White (1937) by Claudette Colbert.

Of course, it's not hard to see why the arrangement changed. Like everything else in Hollywood, it was done for money, the premise being that even though these animated features are kids' fare, marquee stars would appeal to the parents and draw bigger audiences. But is that even true? If the kids begged to see "Ice Age," would parents refuse to take them unless they were assured a "real" movie star was in it? No, absoluetly not.

More puzzling, if increased revenue was the goal, why not look for ways to *cut* costs, rather than raise them? You'd think the advantages of using "unknown" voices would be instantly obvious. Besides saving millions of dollars in salaries (Cameron

Diaz and Eddie Murphy *each* received $10 million for "Shrek 2"), there's ample evidence that no-name voices are effective.

Consider: "The Simpsons" became a mega-hit without marquee voices; they did it with good writing and a talented ensemble of relative unknowns. The same goes for "Winnie the Pooh," "Rocky and Bullwinkle," and any number of other cartoons. They used second or third-echelon actors for the voices, and the results were spectacularly—and enduringly—successful.

Not only are lesser known voices more economical, it can be argued that an anonymous voice allows us to embrace the character more fully because we're able to "lose ourselves" in the performance.

Which is more compelling? A cartoon animal with its own distinct personality, or one with Jim Carrey's readily identifiable voice, where we're forced to imagine Carrey sitting on a stool in a recording studio, wearing sweat pants and headphones, reading his lines?

Also, what about spreading the wealth? No one is suggesting Hollywood should be in the charity business, but isn't there such a thing as wretched excess? There are 120,000 SAG members trolling for paying gigs, and at any given time something like 85% of them are out of work.

Does Cameron Diaz (who earned $20 million for the appalling "Charlie's Angels") really need to beat some struggling actor out of a job? And not to be snarky, but Diaz is an ex- model known for her striking looks rather than her acting ability. How can this woman's "voice" be worth $10 M?

I know a person, an actor, who is a tour guide at Universal Studios. He's a master of voices—high-pitched squeaky ones, deep ones, funny ones, scary ones, dialects of all sorts, you name it. He's articulate and has a wonderful sense comic timing. He could have played a caterpillar in "A Bug's Life" (and done it for union scale).

The absurdity of it all became apparent a few years ago, when I rented a copy of "Toy Story," in Spanish. The more I think about this, the more hilarious a non-sequitur it becomes. Although *all* the voices in the movie were dubbed in Spanish, the film's key advertising hook was that it starred Tom Hanks and Tim Allen.

If you happen to come across the Spanish-edition of "Jaws" (which is titled "Tiburon" for "Shark"), you get to see Roy Scheider, Robert Shaw and Richard Dreyfus speaking dubbed Spanish. It's a little distracting, but at least you get to *see them act.*

But the notion that someone can "star" as a voice in a dubbed movie is nonsensical. Even for Tinsel Town, where some weird things have happened—where, in a 1930 production of "Moby Dick," the studio, looking for a romantic angle, insisted the writers provide Captain Ahab with a girlfriend—having the featured star of the movie *not* appear in the movie is pretty farfetched.

The Exception Magazine
2009

THREE COMMON MYTHS ABOUT LABOR UNIONS

> "Anything that can be digitalized can be outsourced."
> —John Sweeney, president, AFL-CIO

Myth #1: Union wages are responsible for companies relocating to foreign countries.

It's not inaccurate to say that some jobs (e.g., manufacturing jobs) have been moved from the Midwest and Northeast to the South in order to take advantage of a non-union environment, a lower standard of living, and less stringent government regulations regarding environment protection and workers' rights. It's a fact. And there's no arguing that unions are partially to "blame" for that. Even auto manufacturers in faraway Japan have heard about the built-in benefits of setting up shop in the American South; that's why they install their factories down there.

Replacing a union forklift driver earning $17.50 per hour in Cleveland, Ohio, with a non-union driver earning $10.50 per hour in Tuscaloosa, Alabama, might be enough of an inducement for a factory owner to pick up stakes and relocate to Dixie, particularly if he had a large number of employees. Moreover, there's not much a union can do about these wage differentials, other than try to organize as many sites in the South as possible, in order to level the playing field.

But a company that moves its operation to a foreign country isn't doing it to avoid paying a *union* wage; it's doing it to avoid paying an *American* wage. Where being able to pay a non-union forklift driver $10.50 per hour instead $17.50 per hour represents an opportunity to trim costs, the prospect of moving abroad is seen as a shrieking bonanza.

Moving an operation to Asia or Latin America is not a case of union vs. non-union. It's a case of a decent standard of living trying to compete with the permanent underclass of a fledgling economy. It's no contest.

And to suggest that it's somehow organized labor's fault that businesses are forced to exploit the foreign labor market is to perpetuate a lie. The United States could go non-union overnight, and you'd still have businesses seeking foreign labor. Why? Because the wage differentials are simply too staggering, too alluring, even compared to work being done in the U.S. for the federal minimum wage.

Myth #2: Union members are sub-standard workers.

Consider the premise for a moment. People can say or think whatever they wish about labor unions (they can accuse them of being anachronistic, out of touch, too powerful, etc.), but they can't deny that, across the board, union jobs typically offer better wages, benefits and working conditions than non-union jobs. The notion that the best paying, most coveted jobs in a community would attract the least competent workers simply makes no sense.

As a general rule, the highest paying and best-benefited employers will attract the highest caliber of worker—whether we're talking about accountants, cooks, college teachers or warehousemen. Think about it. Which warehouse is going to attract and maintain the better shipping checkers—the one that is clean, safe and generous, or the hole-in-the-wall outfit that pays lousy wages and offers little or no benefits?

Also, because a union shop offers better pay, benefits and working conditions, it's going to have many more applicants to choose from, allowing management to pick and choose from the very best candidates, an option the tiny mom-and-pop enterprise won't have.

Still, this notion that union members somehow aren't as competent or hard-working as non-union members has seeped into the national consciousness. Part of it may be because a union contract provides workers with dignity on the job. That doesn't mean they're bad workers; it just means they don't have to grovel or jump to attention when a boss passes by. Part of it may be that a union contract exposes inferior managers. Working within the confines of a union contract

185

requires the bosses to be consistent and attentive, something which some managers (particularly the lazy or dumb ones) aren't capable of.

You commonly hear this work performance slur in regard to the California school teachers' union, where incompetent teachers (rather than a myriad of other obvious factors) are blamed for low test scores. This is a myth that is being propagated by school administrators who don't have the courage or resources to address the root problem. Blaming the teachers is far easier.

If people really, truly believe that union workers are less competent than non-union workers, then they should think twice before calling 9-11 or flying somewhere on a trip. Police, firemen and pilots are heavily unionized occupations.

Myth #3: Union members can't be fired.

As good as union workers generally are, there are occasions where they, like anyone else, deserve to be fired. And, despite the myth, union members do get fired. Indeed, union members in this country get fired every day, for every manner of violation, from insubordination to poor work performance to insurance fraud to chronic absenteeism (the most common offense).

No contract in the world is going to include language that forbids management from firing a substandard employee. Again, all one needs to do is consider the premise. What management representative would ever sign a contract that contained "immunity" language of that sort? And what union rep, no matter how bold or arrogant, would dare suggest that such restrictive language be written into it? In truth, no one wants to work with deadbeats . . . not even other deadbeats.

Is it harder to fire a union worker than a non-union worker? Yes. Thank god, yes. Having a modicum of job security is one of the virtues of being a union member. Where a boss in a non-union shop might be able to fire an employee because, say, he didn't like his "Nader for President" bumper sticker, or because he wanted to give the job to his wife's nephew, he couldn't do that in a union shop, because in a facility governed by a union contract you need actual *grounds* to get rid of someone.

Again, it's school teachers who are frequently scapegoated here. Administrators complain that it's inordinately hard to fire an incompetent teacher, even though, per the provisions of the union contract, the school has *two full years* from a teacher's date of hire to fire him or her for any reason they like, without having to defend that decision. Two years. Compare that window of opportunity to the standard 60 or 90 day probationary periods found in most businesses.

CounterPunch
2008

THE TRUTH ABOUT CATS AND DOGS

There's a well known anecdote involving Stephen Douglas and Abraham Lincoln. After Douglas had given a long, flowery speech during one of their public debates, Lincoln asked the audience a simple question: "How many legs does a horse have?" "Four," the audience answered in unison. "And how many legs would a horse have if you called his tail a leg?" The audience answered in unison, "Five."

"Wrong," Lincoln said. "Calling a tail a leg doesn't make it true."

Unfortunately, that same illogic applies to the startling trend we see in the field of labor relations. Apparently, some seminar creature stood on his hind legs 25 years ago and declared that the time had come for management and labor to recognize that their relationship was no longer "adversarial" in nature, that they were, in fact, both looking to achieve the same goal.

Since then, everyone's been parroting that glib assertion, as if the mere repetition of it makes it true. Moreover, when one tries to suggest that the characterization is not only inaccurate, but, perhaps, part of a deliberate corporate effort to co-opt the labor movement, he's treated—even by some union officials—as a militant or cynic or, worse, a defeatist.

This is not an attack on capitalism, per se. It is no more an attempt to demonize or excoriate the "profit motive" than acknowledging the presence of fangs and venom is an attempt to demonize a rattlesnake. It's simply pointing out the obvious, which is that management and labor clearly do *not* want the same thing. They want two distinctly different things. And it's been that way for, well, a millennium or so.

If management and labor wanted the same thing, Exxon Mobil executives, in the face of record oil profits (more than $10 *billion* in a single quarter), would have instantly sought ways to reward its hourly workers. If both sides wanted the same thing, Exxon execs would have said, "Hey, we really need to share some of this obscene oil wealth we just lucked into."

Another example: When the Big Three automakers were rolling in money, back in the 1960s, the UAW (United Auto Workers) still had to claw and scratch and occasionally go on strike to get the pay raises the membership deserved. As wildly profitable as they were, Ford, Chrysler and GM nonetheless tried their hardest to keep that revenue out of the hands of the hourly employees who helped earn it.

And another example: When a celebrity like Barbra Streisand receives, say, a lucrative recording bonus, does anyone really think she says, "Great, now I'll be able to increase the pay of my gardener, housekeeper and that guy who walks my dog"? No. This is where Barb's Malibu "liberalism" peters out, and her sense of economic self-interest kicks in. The more they make, the more they resent parting with it.

But these observations shouldn't surprise anyone. Corny as it sounds, this is the way of the world: supply and demand, charging as much as the market will bear, and paying employees no more than required to keep them from quitting— these phenomena are *de facto* laws of economics. We're all big boys and girls. We know how it works.

Still, the one thing that sticks in our craws and makes us want to collectively puke is when corporate America pretends it's otherwise. When accountants and executives pretend we're on the same "team," when they preach that labor unions are obsolete and that workers need only trust their employers to look out for them.

By saying we want the same thing, they mean, of course, that we all want and need a stable and profitable environment. *We* need jobs . . . *they* need workers . . . and therein lies the magic of symbiosis. That's why, when a new business enters a community, its public relations people are quick to remind everyone that the company is there to improve the economy by providing jobs.

But businesses do *not* view the workforce as a benefit; they never have and never will. Rather, they see labor for what it is . . . pure "overhead." And in their relentless effort to reduce costs, American corporations are investing billions of dollars in the development of robotics. Demoralizing as it is, they want those remaining jobs that can't be shipped overseas and done by Third World beggars to be done by 'droids.

Now imagine the poor shmuck who just found out he'd lost his job to a Malaysian factory worker (or to a relative of R2-D2), who pleads with his bosses to recall what they'd told him in company seminars—that we all want the same thing and are all on the same team. Sorry, but this guy would be escorted out by security guards and drop-kicked over the front gate (ten years from now, it will be robots doing the escorting).

So, what's all this have to do with labor unions? Can a union prevent jobs from being outsourced or mechanized? Probably not. And Congress certainly isn't courageous or imaginative enough to pass laws that would punish companies for leaving American soil or replacing live people with machines. After all, this is the same craven group of politicians who sneaks themselves pay raises at 2:00 a.m., so as not to draw attention.

However, if 30% (instead of the current 12%) of the jobs that can't be sent overseas or readily replaced with robots were unionized, we'd have an improved, more dynamic economy. We'd have a more equitable economy. We'd have the beginnings of a resurgent middle-class. And, as "noble adversaries," we wouldn't have to hear anymore of that management tripe about being on the same team.

CounterPunch
2008

RE-THINKING THE FILIBUSTER

"If ten or twelve Hungarian writers had been shot at the right moment, there would have been no revolt."
—Nikita Khruschev, 1956

The historical Iraq War Resolution—the legislative justification for America's invasion of Iraq—reached the U.S. Senate on October 11, 2002, and although the measure had already passed the House by a vote of 296 to 133, and was favored to clear the Senate, no one could say how much opposition it would face.

While some boldly predicted a landslide, others cautiously predicted a plurality smaller than the House's. The final tally was 77-23, with twenty-one Democrats, one Independent (Jeffords of Vermont), and one Republican (Chaffee of Rhode Island) voting against it.

Given the "urgency" of the resolution, and the emotional frenzy the public had been whipped into by the Bush White House, one can imagine the Republican reaction had Senate Democrats chosen to filibuster the resolution.

One can imagine the uproar, the *outrage*, had Democrats prevented a vote on the resolution by resorting to a device most Americans still associate with images of unctuous, over-fed Southern politicians stalling civil rights legislation by reading from the telephone book for hours and hours.

The reaction would have been seismic. Indeed, with the 9-11 attacks still fresh in people's minds, a Democratic filibuster—the equivalent of fiddling while Rome burned—would have been regarded as treason. The Republicans could have flown to the moon on the fumes created by depicting the opposition as traitors and political cowards.

Filibusters are back. When Arlen Specter (R-PA) reversed himself on the Employee Free Choice Act (EFCA)—which would make "card check" the law of the land—and announced he would *not* be voting for cloture (even though he co-sponsored the bill in 2005), he deprived the Democrats of the 60 votes necessary to prevent a Republican filibuster.

Specter's defection—along with Dianne Feinstein's (D-CA)—made it a matter of simple arithmetic; the EFCA was doomed. The Democrats aren't expected to reintroduce the bill until 2011, gambling that they'll gain additional Senate seats in 2010. Instead of hunkering down for a counter-offensive, the threat of a filibuster sent them running for the exits.

Which raises the question: Hasn't the filibuster been sufficiently exposed as the chickenshit parliamentary gimmick it is? And if it has, why are the Democrats so reluctant to reveal the Republicans for the political cowards they are?

Polls show that 53-percent of the public approves of the EFCA. The Democrats have the House locked-up, and (with Franken) 59 votes in the Senate. As the *majority* party, why would they let 41 dissenting Republicans dominate them? Even with a solid 58-42 or 57-43 advantage, why would they capitulate?

If Obama's pre-election support for EFCA was sincere—if, deep-down, away from lobbyists and *quid pro quo* politics, he truly favors card check—he should use the bully pulpit and do what presidents have been doing since the dawn of television: take the issue straight to the people.

He should publicly lambaste the Republicans for using obstructionist gimmicks to prevent votes from taking place. Americans get it. They understand winning and losing; they understand that votes don't always go their way. What they *don't* understand, and are unwilling to tolerate, is not being allowed to try.

Obama needs to ridicule the filibuster as gutless and "anti-patriotic." And if Republicans insist on using it, Majority Leader Harry Reid must suspend Senate Rule 22, and demand they engage in a "traditional" filibuster and not a "procedural" version. He has the authority to do that. Call for a quorum and make these people actually read those monotonous, time-killing speeches.

Moreover, the Democrats should video-tape the whole spectacle and turn it into the Mother of All Sound Bites. Capture on film these senators mindlessly blathering away, and intersperse it with historical footage of 1960s politicians filibustering against civil rights legislation, gleefully waving their southern gravy bibs (Confederate flags). Let the footage speak for itself.

If 41 senators can legally prevent the other 59 from voting on critical legislation, there's something very wrong with the system.

CounterPunch
2009

THEY'RE KILLING LABOR UNIONISTS IN COLOMBIA

Even though the Colombian government argues that the level of violence has, in fact, declined, there have been more than 2,500 union members murdered in Colombia since 1985. More than 400 have been killed since 2002, when conservative president Alvaro Uribe took office, and 19 union members and leaders have already been killed this year.

According to statistics compiled by the National Labor School, a research organization located in Medellin, Colombia, of those 2,500 murders, less than 5-percent of the cases have resulted in convictions.

So who is murdering these union members and why are they doing it? Based on media reports and information supplied by human rights agencies, the murders are being committed by right-wing paramilitary groups and "private armies" who suspect labor unions of harboring left-wing activists or sympathizers, or of being infiltrated by left-wing rebels who actively oppose Uribe's conservative government.

In Latin America there is a long and storied history of home-grown leftist opposition to government collusion with Yankee-led business interests. Apparently, labor unions in the rough and tumble country of Colombia are even less popular with Big Business and Big Government than they are in the United States. At least, in the U.S., business and government interests combine to *litigate* or *legislate* a union to death, not murder it outright.

Although no one is suggesting publicly that the murderous rampage is the result of an official, government-sanctioned policy, President Uribe's former intelligence chief, as well as several of his supporters in congress, are under investigation for having associations with paramilitary death squads.

However, with or without government complicity, these murders have lately become such an incendiary issue in both Colombia and the United States that the U.S. Congress has temporarily stalled approval of the U.S.-Colombia Free Trade Agreement, a bill strongly favored by American business groups and pushed hard by President Bush.

Given the pressure applied by corporate interests and the unfortunate history of *all* such free trade treaties being ratified eventually, it's hard to say how long the Congress will continue to oppose the U.S.-Colombia Free Trade Agreement. The traditional, pro-business argument for establishing expanded trade relations with countries with deplorable human rights and labor records has always been that we can do more to remedy the situation by "engaging" these countries than by snubbing them.

Of course, that's a myth promulgated by business interests, designed to convince the government to open up as many consumer markets as possible, no matter what the damn human rights violations and what, if any, progress is ever made to rectify them. While it's true that boycotts and embargoes don't always work, they do, in fact, work sometimes. It was economic pressure that succeeded in convincing South Africa to abandon apartheid.

But for now, House Speaker Nancy Pelosi has characterized the Trade Agreement as "unacceptable," and insisted on further study of the situation. Colombian labor and human rights groups oppose the Agreement on the grounds that (no surprise) it will funnel money into the top echelons, and further exploit and marginalize working people.

Colombia is the United States' strongest ally in Latin America and the U.S. is Colombia's largest trading partner. Until 2006, it had been receiving the third-greatest amount of annual U.S. foreign aid, right behind Israel and Egypt, respectively. In principle, the money the Colombian government was receiving was to be used to fight the cocaine drug trade. In 2006, Colombia slipped to fourth, having fallen behind Pakistan, whom the U.S. began showering with money in an effort to get them to fight terrorism.

If history repeats itself, the U.S.-Colombia Free Trade Agreement will be amended slightly, a human rights "mission statement" will be added to it, a special commission will be set up to monitor Colombia's progress, and the treaty will be ratified. After that, the murders will subside, Colombian businesses will prosper as never before, some union honchos will likely be bought off, and the overwhelming majority of Colombia's working people will see no benefits whatever.

CounterPunch
2008

DEATH THREATS IN THE WORKPLACE

Every year in the United States a number of employees are fired for threatening other employees with violence. Even when the threat is considered "harmless" by everyone involved—fellow workers, witnesses, even the employee being threatened—management treats it seriously.

Given the realities of today's world, no one in authority risks downplaying a workplace threat. When it comes to "zero tolerance" thresholds, this is the gold standard. In virtually every instance, the employee gets fired.

Two generations ago, an angry person might threaten to punch you in the nose. Today, they say they're going to "blow your bleeping head off." Call it progress. Labor union reps—especially those in industrial settings—not only hear all sorts of weird and dramatic stuff, they receive their share of disturbing phone calls, including death threats.

While I've been threatened with lawsuits and challenged to the occasional fistfight, I've never had anyone ring me up and say they were going to kill me. However, I've known union officers who *have* had their lives threatened, and they all say it was an unpleasant experience.

A couple of weeks ago it was widely reported that AIG executives had been receiving anonymous death threats, presumably as a result of stories about their huge salaries and outrageous bonuses. These AIG executives dutifully reported the threats to the police and, in something of a surprise, also shared them with the media.

Arguably, unless you've experienced it firsthand—unless you've had someone threaten to kill you or your family—you can't know how it feels. Even if you're able, intellectually, to categorize the threats as "crank calls," on some level they're going to continue to gnaw at you.

That said, and as cynical as this will sound, we have to wonder if these AIG folks didn't report these "death threats" as a means of seeking public sympathy—as a device to deflect criticism by sending the media off in a different direction.

After all, they had very few options. They couldn't defend AIG's conduct; they couldn't laugh off the financial crisis; they couldn't insist that, despite losses of billions of dollars, they were still entitled to hefty bonuses—at taxpayer expense. In truth, all that was left was to say, "Help! People want to kill me!"

Some years ago I was part of a union negotiating team that, after months of bargaining, called a strike. We shut the plant down at noon on a Monday, put 700 workers on the bricks, and stayed out for 57 difficult days, right in the middle of a hot, Southern California summer. It was tough. Any strike that lasts longer than five or six weeks is going to get hairy, and ours was no exception.

On about the 40th day (health insurance expired after a month), I began receiving telephone calls. While no one explicitly threatened to harm me or my family, they did say, "We know where you live. Don't make us come there and do something we don't want to do." The words were uttered ominously. Moreover, many people *did* know where I lived.

But given the circumstances, I interpreted the calls *not* as threats, but as the product of frustration and desperation. Because no one (including the negotiators) had a clue as to when the strike would be over—and because tempers were short and nerves frayed, and people were being asked to walk picket in 100-degree heat—a disgruntled union member making a dumb phone call not only wasn't out of the question, it almost made sense.

Also, hasn't experience taught us that people who go to the trouble of making threats aren't the ones who follow through on them? Typically, rattling someone's cage by making a death threat is the full extent of their commitment. It's the guy who never talks about it, the guy you've never heard from before, who presents the real danger.

That's why when you read about people "snapping"—murdering half a dozen people, then killing themselves—you don't hear witnesses say that they'd always suspected the guy would do something like this, or that the he'd always threatened to do it. Rather, you hear the opposite; people say what a nice guy he was, a quiet guy who kept to himself, and how this violent act was incomprehensible.

In real life, deranged people murder their bosses and co-workers; they murder their ex-lovers, their estranged wives, and their estranged wives' boyfriends. They kill total strangers. They even assassinate presidents. What they don't do is hunt down overpaid accountant executives who are responsible for raising our taxes and increasing the national debt.

Again, I'm not trivializing death threats. But I am suggesting that this whole AIG "death threat" story reeked from the very beginning. Bernie Madoff is still breathing air. That alone should tell us these AIG guys aren't going to be touched.

CounterPunch
2009

MANAGEMENT'S DIRTY LITTLE SECRET

For obvious reasons, no company is going to want its employees represented by a tough, effective labor union. No company is going to want its employees represented by a vigilant organization dedicated to improving wages, benefits and working conditions by any means necessary. What management team would welcome something like that? And who could blame them for not?

But given the choice between having no union at all, or having a weak, ineffective, largely *symbolic* one—one with no stomach for a fight, one that lacks the confidence and respect of its own members—many companies have come to appreciate the virtues of the latter.

Companies have found that a union is often the perfect "buffer" between management and the hourly workforce. A union deflects a lot of stuff that would otherwise land on management. Employees who would normally take their gripes and criticisms to their bosses, now have a union to go to instead; and because most of those complaints don't reach the stage of becoming formal grievances, or issues that require action, the union serves as an effective filter.

But more than that, the union also plays the role of whipping boy. By some weird, inverted logic, the membership will hold the union responsible for stuff outside its ultimate control. Perhaps it's the union's visibility and accessibility; but whatever the reason, the membership often blames it, rather than management, for any bad news that happens to come down the pike. It's a strange dynamic.

An example: Following contract negotiations, when the members don't get the wage increase they expect, or find out that a key benefit is being taken away, it's not uncommon for them to blame the union. Blame the union for not getting them a raise, rather than blaming the company for not giving it to them. Blame the union for being unable to prevent losing a benefit, rather than blaming the company for taking it away. A strange dynamic..

Similarly, on the company side, a lazy or incompetent management team has its own convenient uses for a union.

For one thing, it provides a whole range of built-in excuses. The union can be blamed for every manner of screw-up. Weak managers tell their bosses that restrictions imposed by the union contract were responsible for everything from production fiascoes, to scheduling problems, to tying their hands in personnel matters. However, deep down, they know that having a union around can be a blessing. Example: When employees approach management with one of those messy he-said/she-said disputes, management simply defers them to a union rep. They pass the buck. They dump the problem on someone else. It's one of the benefits of having a union shop.

For another, the union is there to share the pain. Take the recent landmark pact between General Motors and the UAW, which takes the administrative responsibility for the hourly health care plan out of GM's hands and gives it to the union. Such an arrangement is unheard of.

Over the last quarter-century the UAW has lost, literally, hundreds of thousands of members. What was once, arguably, America's most prestigious labor union has been ravaged. But along with the sheer numbers, the UAW has, unfortunately, also lost much of its credibility with the membership. To the extent that it has become not only the messenger delivering bad news, but the perceived *co-creator* of that bad news, the UAW has come to be seen as management's "accomplice."

Of course, as far as the company is concerned, things are peachy. They now have the best of both worlds: a labor union that's too weak and fangless to do battle, but one that (as the nominal representative of the employees) is still in the line of fire, still there to take the flak when things turn sour. In a word, the perfect buffer.

And now that the UAW has been saddled with the staggering responsibility of administering the hourly health plan, the union risks moving to the next step in the declension—going from buffer to *scapegoat*.

Just wait until the health insurance issue hits a major snag and things turn ugly. Management is going to thank their lucky stars that they have a union to "protect" them.

CounterPunch
2008

SAG SHOULD BE PRAISED, NOT ASSAILED

On Friday, April 17, after nearly a year of negotiating, a humbled and restructured Screen Actors Guild (SAG) reached tentative agreement with the Alliance of Motion Picture and Television Producers (AMPTP) on a two-year contract. The following Sunday the 71-member board voted to recommend the agreement to the membership.

This contract is said to be no better than the one that's been sitting on the table since last summer and virtually identical to the one accepted by Hollywood's writers, directors and competing actors' union, the American Federation of Television and Radio Artists (AFTRA).

Because the original team (headed by SAG president Alan Rosenberg and chief negotiator Doug Allen) couldn't get the deal it wanted, Hollywood is now piling on, accusing the previous leadership of having under-estimated the Alliance, misread its membership, and failed to anticipate the recession. Indeed, people are now saying the negotiations were an exorbitant waste of time and money.

Those people are wrong.

First, to criticize SAG for not accepting essentially the same contract that was accepted by the writers, directors and AFTRA is to miss the point. Yes, the WGA (Writers Guild of America) signed the contract, but they had to be dragged kicking and screaming to the table. Don't forget: They took a 100-day strike to *avoid* signing it.

Why did they strike? Because the AMPTP's offer didn't adequately address critical issues, including New Media jurisdiction—an area which happens to be (along with residuals) one of SAG's key agenda items. And Rosenberg's committee believed the Alliance's "last, best and final offer" was still inadequate. Second-guess them all you like, but don't say they were wrong for wanting to secure the membership's future.

Second, a quick look at the dynamics of contract negotiations tells us that there are two (and only two) considerations that matter: *fairness* and *attainability*. Obviously, what is deemed "fair" is subjective and is going to depend, by and large, on where you're sitting. What's fair to the union may not seem fair to management. That's why you bargain.

As for "attainability," that can never be known in advance, because a union never knows what can be gotten until it sits down at the table and tries to get it. Bargaining is not about sharing new ideas or reaching a consensus; it's about trying to get very powerful and selfish people to part with their money.

Also, it's important to remember that if organized labor had routinely accepted management's "last, best and final offer"—if they took as gospel management's assurance that such-and-such was simply *unobtainable*—we'd still be working 12-hour days with no health insurance or overtime premiums.

Third, management will use any excuse to avoid sweetening the pot. When there's a recession, they'll use the recession; when there's a hurricane, they'll use the hurricane; and when the economy is healthy and everyone is prospering, they'll give you ten reasons why that prosperity is irrelevant to your negotiations.

And finally, the union knows what to expect. It knows that taking a hard line can be tricky, especially if management chooses to take an equally hard line. On one side, you have management, fully mobilized and dug in; on the other, you have your usual mix of union people: loyal members ready to battle, puzzled members wondering what's going on, and nervous members ready to abandon ship at the first sign of trouble. It's Negotiations 101.

Similarly, union bargainers will be regarded as either weak and gutless, or belligerent and stubborn. Unfortunately, there's very little middle-ground. If a negotiating team puts the membership in jeopardy by asking for a strike vote, they're militants; if they bring back a lousy contract and recommend ratification, they're wimps.

So let's get it right, people. Labor relations is a contact sport. Unless you take the view that your union should *never* fight, or that it should fight *only* when it's assured of winning, you're always going to risk having your butt handed to you in a sling. But if you're not willing to fight for a decent contract, you don't deserve one.

And not to rehash the past, but if SAG's membership had remained faithful—if some of its big-name stars had not seen themselves as deputy ambassadors, and set off on their own bizarre, diplomatic mission—this bargain might have turned out differently.

Actually, it's not over yet. SAG's membership could still reject the offer, which would put the AMPTP in a bad spot. The Alliance can posture all it likes, but a membership rejection, particularly after a board recommendation, would be a body-blow.

CounterPunch
2009

SHOULD UNIONS STOP TRYING TO BE SO NICE?

Maybe it's time for labor unions to arbitrarily assume that any plan introduced by management will likely have a negative effect on the workers. Maybe organized labor should quit playing ball with management altogether, just stop cooperating. In a word, maybe unions should, as Nancy Reagan famously suggested, Just Say No.

In truth, little has come from labor's attempts to make nice. Take, for example, the Democracy in the Workplace campaign of the 1980s. Using as its template the Japanese employer-employee relationship (the one reputed to be kicking our butts in the marketplace), American businesses urged unions to think "outside the box," to open themselves up to a whole new philosophy regarding the way we do business.

Dr. W. Edwards Deming, the statistician and ergonomics expert credited with having "invented" the postwar Japanese business model, traveled the United States conducting seminars and hawking his book ("Out of the Crisis") on how to save the American economy. Japan was clearly on the ascendancy, and we were rapidly falling behind.

Management gushed over Deming's innovative 14-point program for improving efficiency, and unions were quick to buy in to his refreshingly pro-labor stance, where workers on the floor were given an opportunity to participate in the decision-making process, share in the profits, and be treated as "equals."

Of course, what happened was hideous and predictable. Management degraded Deming's philosophy by implementing only those parts of it that benefited them in the short-term, and rejecting anything that cost money or resembled "joint-ownership" of the workplace. Because they'd always feared and resented unions, they hoped that "going Japanese" would be an opportunity to neutralize them.

Democracy in the Workplace turned out to be more hype than substance. It took the form of grassroots employee committees which, predictably (and with the company's urging), ignored or sidestepped the elected union leadership. Not that there's anything wrong with employee involvement; in fact, having a majority of the workers genuinely involved in day-to-day activities is a positive force.

But in many cases these ad hoc committees were free-for-alls, with management offering rewards to the weakest, most pliant workers on the floor as payment for supporting company initiatives. This was "democracy" in its least attractive form. Ironically, when it came time for some really *serious* decision-making to be done, even these company stooges were brushed aside, particularly when their suggestions conflicted with management's master plan.

The mid-1980s and early 1990s turned out to be a period of massive layoffs. Because cutting the workforce was now a priority, Deming's subtle managerial philosophy had been clumsily reduced to an aggressive, unremitting drive to lower head counts. By the time the smoke cleared, and the Democracy in the Workplace movement had petered out, employee rolls had been slashed, unions had been weakened, and company profits had soared.

And then, quite suddenly, the so-called "Japanese Miracle" was relegated to yesterday's news. As other emerging Asian markets arrived on the scene and began competing with Japan, the vaunted Japanese model lost a bit of its luster. Today, if you suggest emulating Japanese techniques, you'll elicit yawns. China is the world's new economic hero. Fortunately, its bizarre mixture of bureaucratic Communism and rapacious turbo-capitalism isn't available for export.

Another example of a bad idea was NAFTA (North American Free Trade Agreement). This treaty has been with us now for 14 years, and, while the jury is still out on some of its long-term effects, it's obvious that the wildly optimistic predictions were mistaken. NAFTA was supposed to create jobs for American workers; instead, nearly 3 million manufacturing jobs have been lost.

Additionally, NAFTA was supposed to help the Mexican economy to such an extent—create so many new jobs in Mexico—that immigration into the U.S. would be reduced to a trickle. Instead, not only has immigration to the U.S. increased, but Mexican farmers have been devastated by U.S. government subsidies to agribusiness, and workers at the *maquiladoras* (border factories) have been laid off or had their wages drastically cut.

So who profited from NAFTA? No big surprise. It was the most powerful business groups in the three countries privy to the arrangement: Canada, Mexico and the U.S. President Clinton's chief economic advisor, Robert Rubin (formerly of the financial giant Goldman Sachs), was a personal friend of Carlos Salinas, the wealthy former president of Mexico. NAFTA was a classic "inside job," initiated and orchestrated by the Republican Party and signed off by Clinton and congressional Democrats too timid and short-sighted to oppose it.

But the best (worst) example of a management enterprise that hurt unions was the swapping of priorities in contract negotiations, which began in earnest during the 1990s and continues today. In order to hang on to their precious health care and pension benefits, unions were persuaded to put off (or even give back) wage increases. With benefits in jeopardy, unions were willing to sign contracts that swapped short-term purchasing power for long-term security.

The central flaw in this strategy was that it had no brakes. Once the unions agreed to forego wage increases in return for maintaining their benefits, management's next move was swift and predictable: they came after the benefits. The unions' voluntary waiver of wage increases served no purpose; health care and pension benefits continued to be eaten away. In the end, unions wound up losing both wages *and* benefits.

The same applied to the two-tier wage format. Reluctantly, unions agreed to sign contracts that included two-tier wage structures (a configuration where new hires are locked into a *permanently* lower wage schedule than senior workers) in return for hanging on to their medical and pension coverage. A case of ideological integrity being sacrificed for long-term stability.

This "selling out" of future employees was an extremely tough call for the unions, a trade-off they agonized over. To their credit, many locals refused to go along, even though they were under enormous pressure to do so. For those who did agree, as soon as management had that two-tier wage provision under their belt (and despite assurances that it wouldn't happen), they began cutting into the very medical and pension benefits the union had sold its soul to preserve. It was ugly.

So what's the answer? If going the extra mile, meeting management more than halfway and expecting them to do the right thing, isn't the solution, then what is? One suggestion might be that labor needs to move in the opposite direction. Instead of détente and mutual cooperation, a harsher, more "primitive" approach may be what's needed.

If accommodating management has lead to treachery and deceit, maybe resorting to strikes, more strikes, lawsuits, and calling management's bluff at every turn would be the more effective tactic. Something needs to be done to back them off. Even if that means going to war. Given all the bitter medicine unions have been forced to swallow over the last 25 years, what have they got to lose?

CounterPunch
2008

THE MINIMUM WAGE REVISITED

"The greatest anti-poverty program ever invented was the labor union."

—George Meany

In 1938, the first federal minimum wage was established. It was set at 25-cents per hour. Not surprisingly, business groups and industrialists protested strenuously not only at having to pay so exorbitant a rate, but at the federal government's naked attempt (as they saw it) to "Stalinize" the American economy.

The next year, 1939, the minimum was raised to 30-cents. By March of 1956, it had crept up to a landmark $1.00 per hour; in May of 1974, it reached $2.00; and by the time Ronald Reagan took office, in 1981, it had risen to $3.35. Notably, it was under President Reagan that the ratio between the minimum wage and the average worker's wage began to grow.

Today, although the federal minimum is $6.55, the gap between the minimum wage and the wage of the average worker continues to widen. In 1968, the minimum wage represented 53-percent of the average worker's hourly wage; by 2006 it had dropped to 31-percent—this despite the fact that the average worker's wage, in real dollars, had, itself, declined significantly.

On July 24, 2009, the federal minimum will be raised by seventy cents, to $7.25 per hour. Let's do the math. Under the *new rate*, if you work eight hours a day, five days a week, fifty-two weeks a year, never take vacation or miss even one day due to illness or family emergency, you will earn $15, 080.

After state and federal taxes, social security, FDIC, et al, have been deducted, it's hard to say how much actual cash you would take home, but, obviously, since what you started with was so little, what you're left with won't be much. Moreover, that $15,000 pre-deduction figure could be more wishful thinking than economic reality, as many of those full-time, 40-hour a week jobs have dried up. Thirty-hour a week jobs are becoming more common.

Some people—libertarians, hope-to-die conservatives, free market fundamentalists—believe we shouldn't have anything remotely resembling a federal minimum wage, that the supply-and-demand dynamics of the marketplace should be the sole arbiter.

On the other side, you have progressives saying that, if you're going to institute such a thing as a *minimum wage*, the least you can do is make it realistic: Make it the *minimum* income on which an average person can actually live.

Arguably, a minimum wage that doesn't supply the necessary *minimum*—doesn't allow one to make the barest living—is more a mathematical construct, a "gimmick," than a living wage. As the Unitarian Church aptly summarized it, "the current federal minimum [wage] is a *poverty wage*, not an *anti-poverty* wage."

But if we're talking about a living wage, what would that *minimum* be? By definition, wouldn't it have to be the amount required for a single person to live independently at what is, more or less, a bare subsistence level: a tiny apartment, transportation to and from work, utilities, food, toiletries and clothing?

While one might be able to pay for "luxuries" such as DVD rentals, cable TV, the Internet or telephone, it's unlikely a minimum wage earner could afford a car, car insurance or car maintenance. Needless to say, health insurance is out of the question. And, if you start adding dependents to the equation—if you're a family with kids, or a single mom requiring child-care—you can forget about it.

Some would argue that the aforementioned scenario is too bleak and despairing. They would argue that, to be able to purchase material goods, people don't necessarily have to be able to *afford* those goods. They don't need a commensurate income. All they require is credit. Unfortunately, there's a rebuttal to the argument that free and easy credit has no downside, and it can be expressed in two words: Brutal Recession.

Which brings us to organized labor. People need to be reminded that America's most prosperous period, the post-war 1950s (and into the '60s), happened to be the same period when the greatest number of America's workers—approximately 35-percent—belonged to labor unions. Was that a coincidence?

When we say "most prosperous," we're not speaking of the wealthiest Americans (the top 2-3-percent), those who are doing far better today than at any time in the country's post-war history. Rather, we're talking about the middle-class, the vast segment of the population that was thriving in the 1950s—who could not only *buy* material goods, but could actually *afford* them. Unfortunately, that same middle-class began shrinking under the Reagan administration and, alas, has continued to shrink.

A proposal: Instead of relying on an artificial device called the Federal Minimum Wage (intended to insure that low-wage workers "maintain contact" with the economy), why not keep the Feds out of it entirely? Why not look to labor and management to reach an equilibrium?

Instead of mandating government minimums which don't—and never will—provide an actual *living wage*, we should allow what conservatives themselves call the "inherent wisdom" of the marketplace to prevail. Allow management and labor to sit down at the table and trust the "wisdom" of the collective bargaining process to lead them to the Promised Land, to a wage/benefit package suitable to both.

It goes without saying that for this arrangement to be effective we'll need more labor union members, because what used to be a robust 35-percent now stands at a puny 12.4-percent. The benefits of union membership should be readily apparent. All one has to do is look around and survey the condition of our "union deficient" landscape.

There's always been this nagging belief out there that labor unions are somehow *bad* for the economy. That's a myth. It's corporate-sponsored propaganda. Unions might be a threat to management autocracy, and harmful to management *greed*, but they're certainly not harmful to commerce. Indeed, commerce loves them.

Economists and progressive business groups (yes, *business* groups) have acknowledged that higher wages help the economy by increasing the purchasing power of the consumers. After all, who's going to buy the stuff available, if the number of flush consumers keeps diminishing? As George Meany famously said, "The greatest anti-poverty program ever invented was the labor union."

It's also been demonstrated that higher wages (union wages) result in greater productivity and lower employee turnover. It's an undeniable fact: good pay and good benefits attract a higher caliber of worker than lousy wages and lousy benefits.

So, besides supplying businesses with more qualified, more stable employees, labor unions create more personal wealth across-the-board. Those bumper-stickers you still occasionally see aren't lying: "Live Better. Work Union." It's true.

CounterPunch
2009

LABOR UNIONS AND TAFT-HARTLEY

Polls show that upwards of 50% of working people say they'd be interested in joining a labor union, but only 12% of America's workforce is unionized. Even acknowledging that some of those expressing an interest in joining up were fooling themselves and misleading the pollster, there is still a huge number of working people out there who would like to become union members but either don't quite know how to proceed or, frankly, are too frightened to make their feelings known, fearing management retaliation.

This discrepancy (between the number of those who'd like to join and actual membership) reflects brutal two truths: management has the statutory ability to limit organized labor's power; and companies are still dedicated to the point of obsession to keeping non-union workers away from union organizers.

While insuring that the workforce remain unrepresented has always been a cat-and-mouse game, one which management has played well through the use of flattery, deceit, rewards and intimidation, the statutory limits on labor's power are directly traceable to the Taft-Hartley Act, passed in 1947. The Act was passed by a Republican congress, with the help of southern Democrats ("Dixiecrats"), over the veto of President Truman.

Taft-Hartley not only amended or rescinded many of the bedrock components of the 1935 National Labor Relations Act (commonly known as the "Wagner Act"), it more or less defanged the labor movement. It domesticated the movement. By adopting a set of "unfair labor practices" (ULPs) that applied to unions in the much the same way that the Wagner Act applied ULPs to management, Taft-Hartley effectively blunted labor's ability to resort to "radical" action.

Taft-Hartley outlawed the closed shop, eliminated the sanctity of the union shop (allowing "right-to-work" states to exist), enacted a mandatory waiting period before calling a strike, made it illegal to engage in jurisdictional strikes, secondary strikes and boycotts, gave management the right to stall and impede a membership certification vote, and expanded the NLRB's governing board from three to five members. In a word, Taft-Hartley made unions infinitely more "controllable."

Right-to-work laws allow employees the privilege of choosing whether to join or not join a union. Prior to Taft-Hartley that right didn't exist; if you hired into a facility that had a union you were required to join it, or you lost your job. Today there are 22 states with right-to-work laws on the books, mainly in the Deep South and Midwest, and four of them (Arkansas, Arizona, Florida and Oklahoma) include these right-to-work provisions in their state constitutions.

Supporters of right-to-work statutes tend to be anti-collectivist, libertarian wannabes who elevate personal choice to iconic status, and are willing to be paid less and accept substandard benefits in return for the right not to have to join a big, bad workers' collective. When you consider the simple arithmetic involved, this antipathy to unions, this flat-out rejection of economic advancement via strength-in-numbers, isn't merely irrational, it's pitiful.

Then, of course, there's the whole other matter of "free riders," those workers who benefit from union wages and benefits by hiring into a union shop but who aren't required to join the union. They're able to maintain their ideological "amateur status" while simultaneously drawing a professional wage. Not too shabby.

Also, it's no coincidence that the overwhelming majority of states with right-to-work laws have significantly poorer safety records than those without them. Say what you will about labor unions, their safety records have always been demonstrably superior to those of non-union facilities, and this has remained true even after passage (in 1970) of OSHA.

Since the enactment of the Taft-Hartley Act there have been a few half-hearted attempts at repealing all or parts of it, most recently under the Carter and Clinton administrations. Vehement Republican opposition and tepid Democratic support were responsible for the defeat of these attempts. There are simply too many lobbying groups opposed to it, too much money arrayed against it, to give anyone hope that the Act will ever be repealed.

But what would the country look like if that were to happen? How would repeal of Taft-Hartley affect organized labor?

In truth, it could be argued that too much has occurred in the intervening 60 years to result in the radicalization of the labor movement. The connection to labor's revolutionary ideological roots has been severed. The face of the American worker isn't what it was in 1947.

Yes, without Taft-Hartley there would be more national membership drives, more people being allowed to join unions, all of which would be a salutary, democratic effect of repeal, one that would benefit working people. But, arguably, the country Is too "grown-up," too cynical and world weary, to engage in radical industrial actions such as secondary strikes and boycotts, even if they were made legal.

With so many workers now invested in the stock market, and union expectations and identity having been profoundly warped over the last half-century, it would be hard to find a critical mass willing to engage in the more radical actions made available by repeal of Taft-Hartley. In any event, to get back anything close to the mindset labor once had would require a lengthy period of adjustment.

Synthesis/Regeneration
Fall, 2008

WADING THROUGH THE GRASSROOTS

We all remember Caroline Kennedy's aborted and somewhat embarrassing pursuit of that New York Senate seat—the one that was vacated by Hillary Clinton when she became Secretary of State, and ultimately filled by Kirsten Gillibrand. Oddly, Caroline's campaign reminded me of a couple of screwball election episodes that occurred some years ago in the labor union I used to work for.

It's been widely speculated that the only reason she threw her hat in the ring in the first place was because Ted Kennedy had pressured her to do it. According to reports, Senator Kennedy, the family's revered patriarch, wanted to make sure there would be a "Kennedy" in the U.S. Senate when he retired, someone to carry on the family tradition.

Unfortunately, Caroline was naïve enough to believe that all she had to do was go on television, remind people of her ties to Camelot, and the gig was hers. Alas, big-time politics don't work that way (something Uncle Ted should have warned her about). Instead, as we all witnessed, her "She Stoops to Conquer" routine didn't play well in New York—not with the electorate and not with the state's power brokers.

Personally, I was sympathetic. I didn't fault her for thinking the job was hers simply for the asking. Given that the lightweight George W. Bush got elected and then *re-elected* to the highest office in the land, I can understand why Caroline would believe the only thing that mattered was the family name. After all, isn't that how political dynasties are born?

The first union incident occurred in the early 1990s, and involved choosing a department shop steward. On the eve of the election, "Greg," vice-president of Local 672 and the officer in charge of recruiting stewards, found himself without a candidate for swing-shift. To everyone's surprise, the incumbent steward had, at the last minute, chosen not to seek re-election, and no one had come forward to take his place.

Shop steward was an important and woefully underappreciated job. Each department—manufacturing, lab, materials handling, stores, infant care, converting, and maintenance—had a minimum of one steward per shift. Not having one on swing-shift was going to be a problem, not only for the production crews who used their steward as a sounding-board and confidant, but for the shift-supervisor who regularly huddled with him when confronted with a knotty problem.

Union by-laws gave the Executive Board the choice of appointing stewards or holding an election, and, typically, the Local would hold an election if there were more than one candidate. But since the early 1980s, the number of people interested in serving as steward had declined so sharply it was hard enough attracting qualified volunteers, much less a full slate for an election. Too much work, too much hassle, too little glory—those were the reasons given for the shortage of takers.

With no one willing to step up, Greg approached "Fred," a swing-shift machine operator, and more or less begged him to take the job. Fred was a good talker and cunning thinker, and, in fact, had been a department steward many years earlier, so he knew the job and was familiar with the union contract. Fred's only problem was popularity.

To put it bluntly, the crews didn't care for him. Some thought he was arrogant and condescending, others considered him too lazy and gutless to stand up to management, and others thought he was just "weird." Not to discount the crews' opinions, but being shop steward, if done right, is a demanding and thankless job. You're constantly saying No to people who want to hear Yes.

Despite not having been active in the union for almost a decade, Fred agreed to take the assignment, but only on the condition that he be *appointed*. In truth, he was an intensely proud man who feared losing an election and being publicly humiliated by having the results posted on the union's Big Board. He made it clear to Greg that he had no interest—*none*—in taking the job if it meant competing in an election. Greg agreed, and that was that.

But when word got out that Fred was going to be appointed steward, two people immediately came forward and insisted an election be held and that they be allowed to challenge him. That's how unpopular Fred was. Regrettably, Fred's vehement objections to competing in an election had somehow been lost on Greg, because the dumb bunny went ahead and placed Fred's and the other two names on the official ballot.

The next day there was a vote, and what happened to Fred was what very likely would have happened to Caroline had she run in an open election: He got creamed. He finished a distant third. It was humiliating.

A few days later he sought me out, all furious and wounded and full of threats, insisting that he'd been "set up." While I agreed that Greg had screwed up royally and deserved a proper thrashing, there was nothing we could do about it now. It was over and done with. Fred stormed away, vowing that "he would never lift a finger to help this fucking union again," and, true to his word, he never did.

The second episode also involved a steward election, but this one had a happier, if bittersweet, ending. The Quality Assurance Lab was having its annual shop steward election, and the formidable, long-time incumbent, "Gloria," was once again running. An excellent, experienced steward—smart, reasonable, articulate—Gloria usually ran unopposed; and on those rare occasions when she did encounter a challenger, she trounced her.

This time around, a new arrival to the lab, an older woman named "Karen," had decided, basically on a whim, to take Gloria on. She contacted the union and requested that her name be placed on the ballot. Because there were only 15 people working in the lab—all women, and all on day shift—the election was conducted on site, and done quickly. The final tally was Gloria: 14, Karen: 0.

Yes, even Karen had not voted for Karen.

Of course, once word of the vote spread, Karen was needled mercilessly, with people coming up and complimenting her, sarcastically, for the fact that even *she* realized she wasn't qualified for the job.

In her defense, Karen said it had been a mistake. She honestly thought "you weren't allowed to vote for yourself"—harking back to some silly rule she'd heard in elementary school. Give the woman an "A" for integrity. In any event, the Gloria vs. Karen election became part of union lore: the only perfect shut-out in Local history.

CounterPunch
2009

ALL UNIONS MUST DIE

There's no shortage of places to look when searching for the beginning of organized labor's decline. By "decline" we refer not to the drop in national membership rolls (which began in the mid-1960s and hasn't let up), but to the profound decline in labor's influence and credibility. We refer to the conditions that permit unions to look down the road and visualize with some clarity their own death.

Purists say it began as far back as 1947, with passage (by a Republican congress over Truman's veto) of the Taft-Hartley Act, which rescinded or watered down many of the provisions of the historic 1935 National Labor Relations Act (commonly known as the "Wagner Act"), the legislation generally recognized as having ushered in the era of the modern labor union.

For 60 years labor activists have flirted with repealing Taft-Hartley. While some efforts made it as far as the floor of Congress, most broke down in the driveway. Despite a consensus that Taft-Hartley is a hindrance to labor's organizing and bargaining, there simply isn't sufficient interest or muscle to put up a fight, and, given the direction of the country, very likely never will be.

If one wanted to quibble, the vaunted Wagner Act itself could be blamed for setting unions on the wrong course. The ACLU (founded in 1920) cautioned organized labor against endorsing Wagner, arguing that when you acknowledge the government's power to "certify" unions (sanction them, give them life) you tacitly acknowledge its power to "decertify" them. The ACLU urged labor to continue to go it alone (as it had done, fairly successfully, since the 1880s), and tell the feds to look for someone else to certify.

The International Brotherhood of Teamsters takes a more parochial view. They argue that labor's decline started with the Carter administration's deregulation of interstate trucking, a development that transformed the Teamies (the nation's largest and most powerful union at the time) from Lords of the

Highways into just a bunch of well-heeled union goons. Not insignificantly, Carter's move (and President Ford's railroad deregulation legislation before him) helped launch what would become the great race to deregulate the world.

More recently, during his 1984 presidential campaign, Walter Mondale claimed that the snake in the woodpile was Ronald Reagan's abrupt firing of 11,000 striking air-traffic controllers, in 1981. That wildly provocative act served to reinvigorate and re-energize dormant anti-labor sentiment in ways no one anticipated. It was as if corporate America was just waiting for the right moment to wage open war against organized labor, and the president of the United States supplied it. The joke going around was that Reagan (former president of SAG) wanted to turn unionism into union-*wasm*.

Still, as damaging as these anti-union initiatives were, they never succeeded in breaking down the one component management most fears: union solidarity. Through all the disappointments, layoffs, assaults, takeaways, restructures, false hopes and broken promises, the membership, by and large, has remained loyal to the Movement. Happily, nothing is more galvanizing than being systematically brutalized by a powerful authority figure.

But something emerged in the late-1980s that has the potential to be even more damaging to a union shop than anything that came before it. Having concluded that they couldn't destroy solidarity by attacking, isolating or starving it, management seized upon an alternative tactic, one that no one (or few) saw coming. Companies discovered that union solidarity could be broken down from the inside, by corrupting it.

This was done by introducing something called "special assignments." A special assignment is an arrangement where hourly workers are taken off their regular jobs and assigned to non-bargaining, non-supervisory tasks for periods ranging from one week to, literally, several years.

Initially, special assignments were confined to safety and training projects, preparing production manuals, helping decorate the lobby for Christmas, etc. However, as things progressed, as the shift-supervisor and certain clerical positions were phased out, hourly workers began taking over many of the day-to-day administrative duties. As long as a special assignment doesn't involve bargaining unit work, or spill over into what the NLRB defines as "supervisory roles" (issuing work directives, reprimands, etc.), there are no restrictions.

The money was good. While the union contract requires employees on special assignment to be paid their regular hourly rate, it doesn't address the distribution of non-unit overtime (paid at time-and-a-half). As a consequence, management permitted, even encouraged, special assignment people to work as much or as little overtime as they wanted, no questions asked. An hourly worker being allowed to write his own ticket was tantamount to being given double-0 clearance, the license to kill.

Management's argument for establishing special assignments came in three parts. First, they acknowledged that there were production workers with hidden talents who, because of the limitations of their jobs, had no way to display or develop them; second, they quoted studies showing that when you take people off a forklift or prod line and give them a chance to "spread their wings," their outlook improves dramatically; third, they noted that more and more companies were eliminating salaried positions for cost reasons, and looking to the hourly to pick up the slack

With production codes and crew sizes varying from week to week, and hourly employees vastly outnumbering salaried, it was obvious, even to skeptics, that the hourly group offered the necessary flexibility. The management argument made sense. Not wanting to appear obstructionist or stand in the way of improving the membership's mental health, the union gave the plan its tentative blessing. And that's how the Trojan horse entered the city.

Two types of people typically get offered these assignments: the smart, hard-working ones (often the de facto leaders on a crew) who feel they've been "over-qualified" for the drudge jobs they've been doing for years and are eager to improve their lot; and those who are technically proficient but fall into the "whiner, nitpicker, jailhouse lawyer" category.

Incredibly, not only does management turn these former trouble-makers (often the brightest people on the crew and the union's most reliable supporters) into model citizens, they do it almost instantly, and with few props: a computer, a coffee-maker, a swivel chair. Human nature does the rest. Pull them off the floor, put them in an air-conditioned office, and voila!— they forget they ever belonged to a labor union. Not to overstate it, but what's that cliché about giving someone a gun and a badge?

It's bizarre. Barely three weeks into a cushy job and these "radicals" (guys who once wanted to raise the black flag and begin slitting throats) already have photos of their wives and kids on their desk. They take coffee breaks with management folks, eat management food, laugh at management jokes, use management-speak to express themselves (e.g., refer to monumental screw-ups as "opportunities"). It's corporate America's version of the Stepford Wives. The Stockholm Syndrome on steroids.

Of course, the effect on those stuck doing their regular jobs is predictable. Morale plummets. People on the floor resent having their peers being placed "above" them—doing bullshit work and making more money—and they blame the union, not the company, for letting it happen. But even the "have nots," the resentful ones who weren't picked in the first round, begin plotting how to get those plum positions for themselves. And who can blame them? Those jobs are better.

Seeing the writing on the wall, the union tried to negotiate these spots into the progression ladder, make them straight-up union jobs, open to everyone, via seniority. Although the proposal was brought up at every subsequent contract bargain, the company wouldn't budge. They argued that the nature of special assignments required people to be hand-picked. The union had the right to veto a choice, but that was the extent of it.

Moreover, because these assignments fell outside the union's province to provide, the membership now looked to the company as its benefactor. Members saw their union not only as stodgy and ineffective, but in some ways (like when it began filing grievances to scale back the program) as an impediment. Full disclosure: Local union officers have accepted these assignments as well. While this is a disappointment, it's not a total surprise. When the gravy train rolls by, everyone is tempted to jump on.

Special assignments are now epidemic in America. As more union workers run day-to-day operations, and the membrane separating labor and management grows thinner, rank-and-file holdouts are uncertain whom to "fight" and where to go for help when a dispute breaks out. It's a mess. And this isn't just a case of a union spouting its usual pieties, or having its feelings hurt over losing a turf war. It's about the welfare of working people.

Despite the slap-happy job assignments and "team-building" seminars, workers continue to fall further behind. Pensions, health insurance and wages continue to erode, and union members continue to be asked to make monumental concessions. Yet, somehow, management still has these employees eating out of their hand, trying so hard to please their masters—even when many of the perks have been eliminated.

Not unexpectedly, the special assignment overtime that was once so plentiful has been drastically reduced. With "factory apes" (an HR term for them) having been fully domesticated and given a taste of office work, and nobody wanting to go back to their mundane jobs (why would they?), it was now safe to withdraw some of the early inducements. Inevitably, management began taking steps to recoup their investment.

The union was more or less co-opted. When corporations found they couldn't beat the union, couldn't penetrate its core, they infiltrated it. They infiltrated it, found their way to the hallowed place, and extinguished the flame.

Looking back on it, few appreciated or understood just how valuable, how sustaining, that Us. vs. Them, class warfare mentality really was, not until we lost it. Management used to rent us. Now they own us.

State of Nature
2008

David Macaray, a Los Angeles playwright ("Larva Boy," "Americana") and political writer, was a former labor union rep with the AWPPW, Local 672.

Lightning Source UK Ltd.
Milton Keynes UK
23 May 2010

154588UK00001B/40/P